DOING IT
WITH STYLE

DOING IT WITH STYLE

QUENTIN CRISP
and
DONALD CARROLL

FRANKLIN WATTS
New York / London / Toronto / Sydney
1981

Library of Congress Cataloging in Publication Data

Crisp, Quentin.
Doing it with style.

Includes index.
1. Style (Philosophy)
2. Identity (Psychology)
3. Personality.
I. Carroll, Donald, 1940-
II. Title.
BF697.C74   155.2   81-3400
ISBN 0-531-09852-4   AACR2

81-25058

CONTENTS

For Bob and Constance Kaine

Introduction

ON BEING
A STYLIST

EVER SINCE THE DAY OUR distant ancestors looked up and noticed for the first time that some people were blessed with a certain indefinable quality that set them apart from others, that endowed their every act and utterance with a special fascination, we have referred to these people as "having style." Whatever they do, they do it "with style."

Strangely, though, considering the homage we have long paid to this magical gift, style, it still remains largely undefined—indeed, for most people, indefinable. That is not to say that many haven't tried. While some have seen it as a synonym for class, others have described it variously as flair, grace, charisma, panache, or a shifting combination of all of them. George-Louis Leclerc de Buffon, on his admission to the French Academy in 1753, took a rather grand stab at pinning it down. "The style," he proclaimed, "is the man himself." It is a definition more notable for its resonance than its clarification.

More recently, Taki Theodoracopulos attempted to settle the question in an essay for *Esquire* entitled, "What, Then, Is Style?" The essay's subtitle indicates how far he got: "Who knows? But when you see it, you know you've seen it." The author's inconclusive conclusion: "Style is an elusive quality. . . . One either has it or doesn't." Which is true enough, but the same could be said for gonorrhea. Or money. What's interesting is not that one has it, but how one got it.

Does this mean therefore that style, whatever it is, is definition-proof? We do not think so. It is our contention that style is not only definable but, more to the point, acquirable.

We would define it thus: Style is an idiom which *arises spontaneously* from one's personality but which is *deliberately maintained*. Or to put it another way: To be a stylist is to be yourself, but on purpose.

Perhaps it is this seeming contradiction—between spontaneity and calculation, between naturalness and artifice—which accounts for the difficulties people have had in deciding precisely what style is. It probably also accounts for the difficulties would-be stylists have in deciding how they should behave in different situations. Seizing on the calculated aspect of style, they tend to think that being stylish is simply a matter of "puttin' on the style."

True style, however, comes from within. All of the elements, the raw material, of one's style are rooted in one's personality. And *everyone* has a personality capable of becoming the basis of a style. What distinguishes the stylist from other people is that the stylist has been able to identify these elements, organize them, refine them, and formalize them into his own unique and recognizable language of behavior.*

Consequently, before you can become somebody "with

---

* The use of the masculine gender here and elsewhere in the book should not be seen as an attempt to exclude women from the kingdom of Style, but merely as part of an attempt to write straightforward English prose unencumbered by superfluous qualifications.

style," you must first be on good terms with your own personality. In short, you must know who you are.

A STYLIST KNOWS
EXACTLY WHO HE IS

For some reason, the single most crucial aspect of your identity is the one you are most apt to overlook: the fact that you are unprecedented. There never has been and never will be anyone quite like you. That tiny chain of carbon atoms which formed the blueprint of your character can never be duplicated. No one else has ever experienced the world in quite the same way that you do. No one else has ever lived your life. You are a minority of one.

Misguidedly, and tediously, most people try to compensate for this unnerving state of affairs, either consciously or unconsciously, by becoming more like others. The stylist exploits it by becoming more like himself.

However, before you can begin to capitalize on your uniqueness you must have a good idea of what it is that makes you different. In other words, you must know yourself. This may require considerable effort. Self-knowledge is not the easiest thing in the world to come by. But it is the best thing in the world to have.

To gain it, you should start by making an inventory of what you consider your strong points (which are not to be confused with your best points)—those elements of your personality which most forcefully influence your behavior. Are you, for example, *in your own eyes* basically active or passive? Optimistic or pessimistic? Gregarious or bashful? Orderly or chaotic? Serious or frivolous? Robust or delicate? Tall or short? Fat or thin? In sum, what is the truth about yourself when nobody's looking?

Having determined that, you need to find out what

others see when they *are* looking. In all likelihood, they will see things that will surprise you. If, for example, you have gone through life wearing pink glasses, you will naturally think the world is essentially pink, while the world thinks of you only as The Person With The Pink Glasses. You may have always thought of yourself as friendly and outgoing, while the world regards you as strangely nervous and talkative. If you are going to get a true picture of yourself, it is vitally important to take into consideration the perceptions of others.

The best way, the only way, is to observe carefully other people's reactions to you. When they are critical of you, take that criticism seriously—even when it comes barnacled by the dreaded words, "The trouble with you is . . ." They may be on to something. And don't just look at the way people treat you *now*. How have they treated you in the past? How did your parents treat you? What was unexpected (or even unjustified) about that treatment? In what circumstances? How did your brothers and sisters treat you? Your teachers? Your schoolmates? Remember, they all have little fragments of the mirror.

One caveat, though. Never *ask* people what they think of you. The chances are that either they will tell you what they think you want to hear, or they will take the opportunity to prosecute some petty complaint that just occurred to them. Neither offers an accurate reflection of the image you project.

In any case, besides being unreliable, such poll-taking is unnecessary. People will always volunteer what they really think of you. The message may be explicit or implicit, delivered by word or action, but it is always there. If you listen and watch closely enough, you will soon learn what distinguishes you in the eyes of others.

With this information, plus your own assessment of your

most prominent traits, you will be in a position to bring your persona in line with your personality, to codify your behavior in such a way as to emphasize and polish that which is essential to your nature and at the same time to do away with everything that is extraneous or distracting. This means not only tailoring your actions to fit your idea of yourself, but tailoring everything else as well: your clothes, your movements, your diction, your vocabulary, your eating habits, your job. Everything, in other words, that goes into that overall statement about yourself which you will offer to the world, and which the world will call by another name.

That name is Style.

A STYLIST ALSO KNOWS
WHAT HE ISN'T

Perhaps the most dangerous trap awaiting you as an incipient stylist is the temptation to cheat *just a wee bit* in your self-presentation. Not to deceive, but merely to enhance the effect. Say you are noted for your commanding presence. Wouldn't it be even more commanding if you were to add a couple of inches to your height with elevator shoes? Or maybe you are deemed impressive because of your aristocratic demeanor. Wouldn't you be even more impressive if you were to upgrade your ancestry just enough to give you a hereditary claim on your behavior? Maybe you have made youthfulness a key ingredient of your style, and you feel it is being undermined by creeping baldness, or failing eyesight, or wrinkled skin, or a sagging bosom. Wouldn't it be helpful to get a toupee, or contact lenses, or a face-lift, or a breast implant? Or suppose that your style is somehow bound up with money, as for instance in the possession of expensive objects that reflect your expensive tastes. Isn't it permissible to explain away the absence of more such objects by pretend-

ing that you once had more money than you have now, or
that you have a temporary liquidity problem? Or what if
you want to be celebrated for your sophistication and yet
have a compulsive fondness for milk shakes? Wouldn't it be
better to pretend to be a lover of fine wine? And isn't it always a good idea to pretend to be a lover of children, even if
you happen to consider infanticide a suitable form of post-
natal contraception?

No, emphatically. These are not ways of improving your
style, they are ways of *dis*proving it. They are merely disguises, and however perfect you may think they are, people
will see through them. Not that they really need to see
through them, because sooner or later, usually sooner, even
the best disguise will slip a little, if not come off completely,
and whatever style you might have had will be sabotaged by
your pretense.

So *never* pretend to be what you're not. Even by just a
wee bit.

Instead, you should embrace your limitations. Make
them part of your style. If you are basically lazy, don't make
yourself miserable with pointless displays of energy. Follow
Oblomov's example and stay in bed. If reading bores you,
don't spread books and magazines around to advertise your lit-
eracy. Rather, empty your place of all reading matter so that
the world will know that you have lived a life untouched by
the printed word. Likewise, if you are indifferent to the
glories of art, don't inflict pictures on your walls to try to
cover the gaps in your aesthetic appreciation. Instead, banish
from your sight everything suitable for framing.

This is not to say that all of your shortcomings are to
be cherished and paraded before the world. It is quite likely
that some of them will simply be the result of bad habits or
restricted opportunities, in which case you should certainly
feel free to make whatever improvements you think are

needed. For instance, if you suffer from an underdeveloped vocabulary, or an uncertain sense of grammar, you should definitely seek to remedy the problem. The more words you have, and the clearer your understanding of how they work, the easier it will be for you to project your style. It is only when your limitations are an integral part of your personality, or your person, that you should incorporate them into your style.

A STYLIST NEITHER
COPIES NOR COMPETES

Imitation may be the sincerest form of flattery, but it is also the surest sign of stylelessness. And you will see that sign almost everywhere you look. As Oscar Wilde once wrote in a letter to Lord Alfred Douglas, "Most people are other people. Their thoughts are someone else's opinions, their life a mimicry, their passions quotation." He might have added: "And that is why most people lack style."

To be sure, the urge to imitate is a formidable one, and one that strikes early. As children, our need for acceptance by our contemporaries as well as by our parents puts enormous pressure on us to suppress our individuality and try to copy the behavior of those who seem to be more popular or more loved than we are. The effort, of course, is doomed to failure. Worse, it often dooms us to a lifetime of feeling that we somehow don't measure up to "the competition."

It is therefore essential to bear in mind that the stylist never measures himself against others. Such comparisons are not only meaningless but degrading. Consider the example of Mrs. Edward Kennedy when her husband was challenging President Carter for the Democratic presidential nomination early in 1980. After months of keeping her prudently out of the public eye, Senator Kennedy apparently decided that what his campaign needed was a show of connubial happiness, so he reached out and pulled her into the spotlight with him. It was a fatal mistake. Not only did she create a distraction rather than an attraction at a critical moment in the Senator's campaign, but she also took it upon herself to tell the world why she would be better in the White House than Mrs. Carter: She had met more world leaders than Mrs. Carter had, she had studied longer at a university, and so on. Needless to say, she was scarcely seen or heard from after that.

Now the point here is not that she should have kept these fatuous observations to herself. The point is that if she knew who she was—if only she knew whose *wife* she was—they would never have occurred to her in the first place.

This is why the true stylist never compares, never competes, and never copies. He knows that it is fundamentally unstylish to want to be the equal of—or get the better of—someone else. And he knows that to try to imitate someone else is worse than unstylish; it is, quite literally, self-destructive.

Yet most people go on trying, and go on failing. The result has been to create, in a land that once prized "rugged individualism," a sort of edgy conformism that makes every American of a certain age and background seem to foreigners like a bad caricature of every other American of the same age and background. Nor is the situation any better in England. According to John Coleman, writing in the London *Sunday Times,* "It is the perpetual inaccuracy of imitation that makes up the English social comedy and tragedy."

One could amend that to read: It is the perpetual *need* to imitate that makes an *individual* both comic and tragic.

But we should not take this too far. Nobody can expect to have a style that is completely original. Just as even the most revolutionary invention is nothing more than other inventions put together in a new way, your style will inevitably be compounded of elements you have expropriated from the styles of others. The problem is in choosing those—and only those—elements which are emblematic of *your* personality, and discarding everything else. It is very tempting, when constructing a style, to borrow too heavily from a single source —one person's set of mannerisms, for example, or another person's mode of dress. But the temptation must be resisted, or your style will be lost in mimicry. Equally tempting is to think that because something works for someone else it will work for you. This is a delusion. If something works for you it will be because it is the perfect expression of an aspect of your personality, not because it looks good on someone else.

What this means is that before growing a beard, or getting a new hairdo, or changing your wardrobe, or buying a sports car, or using a cigarette holder, or redecorating your house, you have to ask yourself if the contemplated addition or alteration, however small, really echoes something within you. If it doesn't, it will be seen as an affectation. If it does, it will be seen as what it is: a further refinement of your style.

A STYLIST IS CONSISTENT

A few years ago one of the authors had the privilege of spending several hours in the company of the great sculptor Henry Moore at his home in England. As the two strolled through the grounds inspecting the various sculptures on display there, the author asked Mr. Moore if he didn't feel a twinge of sadness when he saw his works go off to be put into museums. No, Moore said, it didn't bother him at all, because "there's no one correct place or right place for a piece of sculpture, just as there isn't one right place, or shouldn't be, for a human being." He went on to say that a person— whether at home, or at a party, or up on the stage—should always be the same person. Likewise, the quality of a sculpture should not change under different conditions. He concluded: "I believe that a piece of sculpture is a bit like a human being; you should be able to tell its character wherever it is."

Alas, Henry Moore's words apply to only a small number of sculptures—those that will stand the test of time—and a small number of people, the ones who have style.

Consistency is the *sine qua non* of style. Taki Theodoracopulos, a man of considerable style himself, was quite right when he wrote of style, "One either has it or doesn't." Period. It is not something that one switches on or off depending on the circumstances or the other people present. It either exists in all situations, or it does not exist at all.

This is perhaps the hardest lesson that the would-be stylist has to learn. To twist slightly T. S. Eliot's memorable line, most of us prepare a face to meet the faces we meet. William James put it more philosophically, if less poetically, in *The Principles of Psychology:* "A man has as many social selves as there are individuals who recognize him and carry an image of him in their mind." He then went on to say that since these individuals tend to cluster into distinct circles, a person "generally shows a different side of himself to each of these different groups."

But why? Why do people feel compelled to play different roles before different audiences? Because they fear that if they don't, they won't get the approval and love they need to sustain their self-image. As W. H. Auden wrote, with poignant honesty, "The image of myself which I try to create in my own mind in order that I may love myself is very different from the image which I try to create in the minds of others in order that they may love me."

To the stylist, such a confession would be incomprehensible, for the stylist neither needs nor seeks the approval of others. He does not view himself as a participant in a popularity contest, but as someone whose carefully preserved uniqueness makes popularity irrelevant, whose style is its own reward.

Take the case of G. Gordon Liddy, the famous burglar, patriot, and volunteer assassin (whose proffered services, fortunately, were not required). It is hard to remember, or even imagine, the emergence of a more thoroughly unattractive character than Mr. Liddy, but the man does have style. As he writes in his autobiography, "I made myself precisely who I want to be"—and he has remained consistently faithful to his own creation. That is to say, he is by his own admission just as loathesome in private as he is in public.

But the last word on consistency belongs to George Bernard Shaw. Toward the end of *Pygmalion,* Professor Henry Higgins passes on this bit of wisdom to his protégée, Eliza: "The great secret, Eliza, is not having bad manners or good manners or any other particular sort of manners, but having the same manner for all human souls."

A STYLIST IS PREDICTABLE

A curious fact: When people are admonished to be consistent in their behavior, they always agree that this is desirable (whether or not they feel it is possible), but when they are urged to be predictable, they usually react as if they have been advised to contract an unmentionable disease. Somehow the notion has gotten around that while consistency indicates strength of character, predictability is a sign of weakness, inferiority, lack of control. It is precisely the opposite.

Predictability is *systematic* consistency. To be predictable is simply to formalize your consistency in such a way that it is instantly recognizable. The old music hall comedians understood this very well; they knew that what the audiences flocked to hear were the same old gags, told in the same old way. Indeed, whenever the performers failed to deliver the lines for which they were famous, the audience would happily do the job for them. Similarly, Johnny Carson—the man who, it is said, has been seen or heard by more people than any person in history—never fails to incorporate into his opening monologue a line like "Boy, it was hot today," just so that his delighted audience can roar back in unison, "How hot was it?"

Westbrook Pegler used to say, "Never sell anything just once. People will think you didn't mean it." Politicians, whose survival in their chosen profession depends exclusively on the public's perception of what they represent, know how true this is because they know that their electability in large part rests on their ultimate predictability. A suddenly unpredictable politician is apt to become, just as suddenly, an ex-politician.

Even so, there are those who ought to know better who still believe that in some strange way unpredictability is a virtue. Not long ago, Gore Vidal told an interviewer from *Rolling Stone,* "One of the problems of being well-known for a long time is that you find yourself doing impressions of yourself." Vidal is too much of a stylist to mean that. What he calls "doing impressions" of himself is really a matter of *being* himself. Repeatedly.

A STYLIST IS SINCERE

In *The Importance of Being Earnest,* Oscar Wilde wrote: "In matters of grave importance, style, not sincerity, is the vital thing." That one sentence explains Wilde's ultimate failure as a stylist. Although he was celebrated throughout much of his career as a man of great style, all along he was concealing a dirty little secret about his style: *He didn't really mean it*. Thus when he was imprisoned for two years in Reading Gaol, after having done everything in his power to promote his incarceration, he was suddenly reduced to a heap of self-pitying rubble, which soon began emitting a trickle of mawkish verses and other sentimental drivel. At the very time when his style should have saved him it abandoned him, because it wasn't anchored in sincerity.

A more recent example of the same phenomenon occurred in the famous television confrontation between Gore Vidal and William F. Buckley, Jr. at the 1968 Democratic convention in Chicago. Here were two men who had both founded their style on a reputation for dry wit, cold reason, and general unflappability. Yet Vidal, normally possessed of an enviable style, let Buckley turn the "debate" into a puerile shouting match full of playground name-calling. Worse still, the two of them kept it up for months afterward, as first Vidal attacked Buckley in an article for *Esquire,* and then Buckley sued Vidal for libel, and then, having won a settlement from Vidal, Buckley gloatingly resurrected the whole affair in his next book. All very messy and hysterical. You had two men who had strenuously cultivated an image of cool sophistication—yet when it mattered most their style deserted them.

Still, despite the fact that the history of style is littered with the bleached bones of those who thought that they could hide behind a distorted image of themselves, as if it were a form of camouflage, many people nonetheless find it difficult to accept that something as calculated as style could be intimately connected with sincerity. There is probably not a celebrity alive who hasn't at some time been told, "If you're not careful, you'll start believing your own publicity." And think of the number of times you have heard someone say of a public figure, "I wonder what he's *really* like."

A stylist is really like exactly what he appears to be like.

He has the same image of himself that everyone else has. His image doesn't mask his true personality, it magnifies it. And a stylist *does* believe his own publicity. To do otherwise would be to make himself a party to a hoax.

And style is not a hoax.

A STYLIST IS CONSPICUOUS

Not long ago an editorial in the New York *Daily News* carried a curious lamentation. "Sad to say," the paper moaned, "it appears we've reached a point in this country when people can make a career just out of being famous." Actually, we reached that point some time ago—as a result of the invention of radio, motion pictures, television, and jet travel. But that is not what makes the statement puzzling. What's puzzling is that the *Daily News* editorial writer was "sad to say" it.

You have to have a lot of style to make a career "just out of being famous." Obversely, you cannot have style if you are marooned on a desert island. A stylist needs people, for his style consists of everything about him that has come to the attention of others. In fact, one of the ways to assess your Style Quotient is to compare the number of people you have heard of with the number of people who have heard of you. A stylist will be known to far more people than are known to him. And the greatest stylists will be known not for what they have made, or what they have done, or whom they have married, but for what they *are*.

One could say, then, that a stylist is someone who is *seen* to have style by a large number of people. Which means that you must be prepared to be as public as possible with your style. British Prime Minister Lloyd George, himself a man of enormous style, summed this up nicely when he told a colleague that "once one has assured oneself of food and shelter, which means security, the next thing that matters is advertisement."

Of course this also means that you must be prepared to forfeit any claim to privacy. For the stylist this is no great sacrifice. He knows that without people around he could no more be stylish than a swimmer could exercise *his* talents without water. So whenever you hear someone complaining about not being left alone by photographers or journalists or fans or the merely curious, you are hearing the complaints of someone sadly lacking in style. Ignore them. Instead, heed the example of Tallulah Bankhead, who became a great stylist, to quote one of her biographers, by "systematically invading her own privacy."

It follows, therefore, that only by populating your life with swarms of people can you ever hope to achieve the level of style of such Old Masters as Tallulah or Lloyd George, whose sense of style was such that John Maynard Keynes once remarked that when Lloyd George was alone in a room there was nobody there.

A STYLIST IS
TRULY LIBERATED

Style is freedom. It is freedom from the need to be competitive, from the need to be fashionable, from the need for "success," from the need for approval. But it is also more than simply freedom *from*. On another level it is a continuing celebration of one's singularity. The French philosopher Henri Bergson summed it up exquisitely: "We are free when our actions emanate from our total personality, when they express it, when they resemble it in the indefinable way a work of art sometimes does the artist."

It should be mentioned that when you have achieved this blessed state—that is, when you have perfected your style

—you can count on having to put up with a certain amount of hostility and criticism. You will have to decide for yourself in each instance whether the criticism is justified or not, and take the appropriate steps if it is, but in most cases you will find that it stems from either ignorance or insecurity. For example, you will almost certainly be accused of being too self-regarding and self-centered. But you should know that it is impossible to be too self-regarding, for the maintenance of your style demands constant monitoring (which in turn requires detachment, and thus is the opposite of being self-centered). So whenever you are confronted with this particular criticism, you should remember the words of the great French diarist Jules Renard. "I find," he wrote, "that when I do not think of myself, I do not think at all."

Remember, too, that any clearly marked personality is bound to arouse some hostility because it is seen as a threat, an implied rebuke to those who are uncertain as to who they are. Merely by being a stylist you will cause some people (those most notably lacking in style) to feel inadequate, and naturally they will resent it. Unfortunately, there is nothing you can do about this. Certainly you should not attempt to explain or justify yourself. As Joseph Addison wrote, "There is no defense against reproach but obscurity."

In any case, for those who have style, criticism is something that comes with the territory. Dean Swift said it best: "Censure is the tax a man pays to the public for being eminent." So be grateful that you are asked to pay it.

Now, having offered our definition of style, and having underlined the most important characteristics of the stylist, one final thing needs to be said before we go on to consider the specific activities and situations in which you will employ your style: *A stylist sticks by his style.* Once you have yourself in focus, you shouldn't fiddle with the knobs. If you do not immediately receive the recognition or elicit the reactions to which you think your style entitles you, don't be tempted to turn up the volume—or to switch it off altogether. It will take people time to recognize and react to your style, because it will take *you* time to develop it and perfect it. This cannot be done overnight, but then you weren't created overnight either.

Franz Kafka once observed, "All human error is impatience, a premature renunciation of method." To the stylist this truth is self-evident. He knows that he is the ultimate method actor, and that he has taken on a lifetime role: playing himself.

DRESSING

with Style

ALTHOUGH IT GOES WITH-
out saying, we will say it anyway: Dressing with style has
nothing whatever to do with being fashionable. Indeed,
fashion (or fashionableness) is the antithesis of style. Fashion
is what is followed by people who do not know who they are,
people who depend on fashion magazines to create an identity
for them.

Your manner of dress constitutes a personal statement
about yourself. It is a message to the world saying who you
are. Moreover, it is the first—and in many cases the only—
message that the world at large ever receives. Therefore,
people who dress according to the dictates of fashion are
passing up a precious opportunity to tell us something about
themselves; all we know when we see them is that they had
enough money to buy the clothes when they came into
fashion.

More succinctly: Dressing with style is akin to issuing a
manifesto; dressing fashionably is like signing a petition.

A quick glance down the street will be enough to tell
you that most people tend to dress either in uniform (to
signify that they belong to a certain group or class) or in
camouflage (to signify as little as possible, in hopes of not being spotted and picked on). The uniform may be that of eco-

nomic rank, such as a business suit—which Marxist critic John Berger has called "the first ruling class costume to idealize purely *sedentary* power"—or it may be some kind of rebel uniform (hippie, punk, or whatever). Either way, except in rare instances, the uniform is worn as part of a *group* statement. It serves to announce your sameness, not your distinctiveness, and thus it is a saboteur of style.

Nor can you hope to establish your individuality by adopting one of the sartorial aberrations currently popular, such as wearing the shirt collar outside the jacket, as popularized by second-rate entertainers on the West Coast, or wearing designer jeans, as popularized by massive advertising, or wearing proletarian fancy dress, as popularized by (of course) the rich. Anything worn because it's popular only blurs your individuality.

This is not to say that you should avoid wearing something simply because other people are wearing it. The stylist wears what is right for him, what is most expressive of his personality. What other people wear is irrelevant.

By the same token, you should never dress merely to be different, because this too involves comparing yourself with others, identifying yourself in terms of others. A stylist *may* be different, of course, even strikingly so. Benjamin Disraeli, a supreme stylist, was a conspicuous dandy at a time when those around him were garbed almost exclusively in black. But he dressed the way he did not because he had something negative to say about others, but because he had something positive to say about himself.

In *Hamlet,* Shakespeare gave Polonius the line, "The apparel oft proclaims the man." This is even truer today now that we have largely abandoned the protocols that once stipulated certain types of dress for certain types of occasions. As we no longer have to dress to show our acknowledgment of an occasion, we can dress to show our *attitude* to the occasion. Indeed, dressing is the most concise way of summarizing your attitudes toward life in general.

Whether you are dressed as a priest or a Hell's Angel, you are letting the world know what to expect from you.

This is so regardless of what you wear or where you wear it. (Although it would appear that some people have been a little slow to catch on to this. Writing in *New York* magazine about the 1980 Cannes Film Festival, journalist Pete Hamill revealed a startling discovery he had made: "In Cannes, clothes were not worn to deal with the elements, but to transmit messages about personality and intentions." Surprise.) At any rate, whether you like it or not, every time you dress you are divulging information about yourself.

You must therefore take care to see that it is the right information. When dressing with style, everything should be of a piece. Everything should complement and elaborate on the central message. As with any statement that you expect to be taken seriously, you cannot afford to contradict yourself. If any sartorial contradictions or non sequiturs are allowed to infiltrate the apparel that "proclaims" you, then your proclamation will be misleading, and your style will suffer accordingly.

That's why it is crucial before buying or wearing any garment to satisfy yourself that it accurately reflects a facet of your character and personality. If it does, then it is right for you, regardless of whether it "goes with" something else that is also right for you. There is nothing wrong with high heels and blue jeans together so long as together they tell the truth about you.

Fortunately, unlike most of the revealing statements that you will make in public, the statement you make with your clothes is one that you can rehearse endlessly in private. And all the great stylists do just that. Noel Coward once told Cecil Beaton, "I take ruthless stock of myself in the mirror before going out. A polo jumper or unfortunate tie exposes one to great danger." Noel Coward knew what style is all about. So, too, does Andy Warhol, who has written self-mockingly: "I have to look into the mirror for some more clues. Nothing is missing. It's all there. The affectless gaze. . . . The bored languor, the wasted pallor. . . . The shaggy silver-white hair, soft and metallic. . . . Nothing is missing. I'm everything my scrapbook says I am."

That is all that matters when it comes to dressing with style—that you and your image are indistinguishable. It matters not whether you dress expensively or cheaply. The Maharajah of Patiala, a name to conjure with in the twenties, reputedly spent upwards of $100,000 a year on his underwear alone, and Diamond Jim Brady once laid out close to that amount for a single set of shirt studs, vest studs, and cuff links. Yet neither had as much style as Laurel Lee, the author of *Walking Through the Fire,* who used to advertise her poverty by always wearing the same long floral dress with a pin. "When I wear the pin," she would explain, "it's a dress, and when I take the pin off, it's a nightgown."

Similarly, as far as style is concerned, no one type of material is inherently superior to any other. It is only when one type *pretends* to be another type that it has consequences for your style. You should never wear anything that pretends to be something it isn't: polyester pretending to be cotton, plastic pretending to be leather, and so forth. To do so is to fall victim to the Margarine Fallacy, which is the curious notion that something is valuable only insofar as it resembles something else. Thus, just as margarine is promoted on the basis of its resemblance to butter, synthetic materials are often judged by how convincingly they imitate "the real thing." In fact, they should be judged exactly as people should be judged—by how convincingly they imitate themselves. And, of course, by how convincingly they represent *you*.

Once you have decided how your style will manifest itself in your dress, that is to say once you have your "look," don't tamper with it. If it is an accurate reflection of your personality today, it will still be so (if not more so) ten, twenty, thirty years from now. This doesn't mean that you have to wear the same clothes for a lifetime; it does mean that you have to wear the same *kind* of clothes. Fidel Castro knew what he was doing when he refused to abandon his green army fatigues after coming to power in Cuba. Mao likewise understood the importance of maintaining his revolutionary wardrobe long after the success of the revolution.

Now compare these examples with that of Marshal Tito. Although Tito was in many respects a greater military and political leader than either Mao or Castro, and although he had enough sense of style to change his name in order to reinforce his image, he made the mistake of trying to apply an overlay of respectability to that image by switching over to sober business suits—and thus he failed to capture the world's imagination in anything like the way that Mao and Castro did.

If dressing with consistency from year to year is one of the hallmarks of a stylist, so is dressing with consistency from situation to situation. A stylist would no more change his mode of dress to suit different circumstances than he would change his signature to suit different people. He always dresses the same—perhaps not in precisely the same clothes, but in the same manner—whether he is at home or at work, in the city or in the country, alone or with others.

Admittedly, certain garments or outfits will be inappropriate in certain situations, but the overall effect should always remain the same. Whatever the situation, you are still the same person, and your clothes should announce that fact.

Tom Wolfe, who probably has more style than any writer in America today, is an excellent example of someone who has mastered the art of consistently matching his clothes to his style. Whatever the occasion, Mr. Wolfe wears a three-piece white suit. Moreover, this distinctive outfit is the perfect equivalent of that distinctive prose style—laced with italics, capital letters, and exclamation marks—which he employs regardless of the subject matter. Indeed, one could say that his suits are textile exclamation marks.

By contrast, Linda Ronstadt exhibits a pitiable degree of confusion in her dress. She will appear in designer boots one day, on roller skates the next, and barefoot the next. She is capable of wearing a silk dress to a beer joint and blue jeans to Nancy Kissinger's presidential inauguration party. Not coincidentally, her musical tastes have changed just as radically, and as often, over the years. She is obviously still trying to decide who she is.

There is one further aspect of consistency in dress that ought to be mentioned, and that is the importance of synchronizing your body language and your dressing language. If you are going to dress more or less formally, you can't afford to flop about. If you are going to dress sportively, you can't mince around the place with dainty little movements. Your postures and gestures must be in harmony with your style of dress, or they will rob your dress of its style.

As to the question of jewelry and accessories, there is no general rule. Obviously, anything that contributes to and sharpens the image projected by your clothes is a plus. Anything that detracts from it, or *distracts* from it, is a minus. There are, however, a few items that no stylist would ever wear. For example, anything that identifies you in terms of a group—an old school tie, a college ring, a Phi Beta Kappa key, a Masonic pin—should be avoided at all costs. The same goes for anything conspicuously bearing a designer's name, initials, or trademark. Your clothes are meant to be an advertisement for yourself, not a commercial for someone's merchandise.

This brings us, finally, to the one aspect of your personal appearance which is not concerned with clothes: your physical attractiveness. What part should that play in your style? The answer is very little.

Personal beauty is at best a mixed blessing. On the one hand, if you are exceptionally handsome or beautiful you are more likely to get decent service in stores, more likely to get picked up when hitchhiking, and, according to a recent study, more likely to get acquitted by juries. On the other hand, great beauty can be a distinct handicap. For one thing, it is apt to arouse envy and mistrust and other emotions which are impediments to your effectiveness as a stylist. For another, it is apt to give rise to unwanted sexual complications. (If such complications are wanted, then you already have a problem with your style.) Worst of all, though, beauty fades. It is the one thing about you that you cannot possibly maintain. So to make it an integral part of your style or, worse, to base your style on it, is a grave error. For when it goes, as it some day will, your style will go with it.

Certainly, great beauty and great style can exist side by side. Tallulah Bankhead is a case in point. While she was never reluctant to accept the advantages that her beauty conferred, she made sure that it remained incidental to her style, which was built on an infinitely more durable foundation. Thus when her beauty faded, her style remained unaffected. She didn't lose an ounce of her *Tallulahness*.

By way of sad comparison, consider the fate of Dorian Leigh, the famous "Fire and Ice" girl of the Revlon advertisements in the fifties. A stunning and vivacious beauty, she was the inspiration for the character of Holly Golightly in Truman Capote's *Breakfast at Tiffany's*. But when her beauty (on which she had staked everything) began to fade, her life came apart at the seams. Now, too late, she tells people that she wishes she could go back and change "every single minute" of that life.

W. C. Fields used to say that he pitied the man who woke up in the morning without a hangover, for he knew that he wouldn't feel any better all day. Much the same could be said about those who begin their lives blessed with great beauty: They know their looks won't get any better, and after a certain point will definitely get worse.

Indeed, one could argue that in the long run the advantage lies with the less well-favored. In the first place, they have a physical advantage because the accumulation of years —which so mercilessly creases, mottles, and tugs at beautiful faces—tends to soften and ennoble the features of the less attractive. And when it comes to keeping their style intact they have an advantage because they will have had to come to terms with their physical limitations early on; there are no nasty surprises awaiting them down the road.

Nonetheless, the question arises: To what extent should you attempt to enhance your attractiveness cosmetically? The answer: To whatever extent you like, so long as the cosmetics are used to tell the truth about yourself rather than to tell a lie about your age. If you wear cosmetics to try to make yourself look younger, you will succeed only in making yourself look like someone who desperately wants to be *thought* younger. Needless to say, this is not the effect that someone with style would ever wish to create.

If you are a stylist, cosmetics are solely a means of bringing out and highlighting something about yourself; they are not for painting over the defects in your facade. For the person with style, cosmetics have only one function: to make you look more like yourself.

Therefore, in choosing your cosmetics, as in selecting your clothes, you must first decide exactly what it is that you want them to say about you. And, too, you must be sure that they don't in any way contradict the message of your clothes. Then, when you have selected the ones you think will do the job for you, you should stay with them. (The same goes for scents, by the way: You should choose the *one* perfume or cologne, if any, that works for you, and then stay with it.) To follow fashion in cosmetics is as demeaning and self-defeating as following fashion in clothes.

What about hairstyling? Here again, the way you wear your hair should be determined exclusively by the statement you wish to make about your style. If you decide that a lavender-tinted pompadour or a pink Afro will add just the right touch to your image, then that's the way you ought to go. But if you want to have your hair dyed blonde because you think blondes are more glamorous, or have it cut short because that may be more fashionable, or have it darkened to hide the fact that you're going gray, then you are in for trouble. Like all disguises, a hairstyle that is at odds with your true self, and consequently with the rest of your image, will eventually betray you.

For the same reason, hairpieces are a bad idea. Quite apart from the fact that they are always more noticeable than you think they are, and the fact that they have an unfortunate tendency to slip out of position at the most awkward times, they have a fundamental flaw in that they were designed not to *reveal* something about you, but to *conceal* something—your baldness. This is of course true of hair transplants as well. However, hair transplants do have two advantages over your ordinary "rug." One is that it is your own hair that is being used. The other is that the relocated hair is attached permanently (most of the time anyway). As against that, hair transplants have a couple of drawbacks that should give anyone pause. First, the operation is an expensive and painful tribute to one's vanity. Secondly and more decisively in any discussion of style, as soon as the word is out about the transplant (which won't be long), your new thatch will become something of an attraction in its own right, drawing attention away from the rest of you. Try watching Frank Sinatra or Jack Nicholson or Elton John without letting your gaze wander up their foreheads. It's difficult—and it interferes with your appreciation of their performance.

Whenever people perceive that there is something about you that doesn't quite fit, that is somehow out of place, they will be distracted by it. And anything that distracts from your overall presence is an enemy of your style.

If you are absolutely and irrevocably convinced that your hair in its present condition is doing you a disservice, it is always a far better idea to embrace and emphasize that which bothers you than to try to cover it up. If you are going bald, have your hair cut (or shaved) in such a way as to proclaim the fact. If you are going gray, accelerate the process by dyeing *all* of your hair gray.

Similarly, if you are persuaded that the only way you can make your appearance reflect your style is by applying artificial color to your hair, it is best to see to it that the color is *recognizably* artificial. If your hair is very obviously or flamboyantly dyed, people will take it as something you want to say about yourself. If it is discreetly dyed so as not to be immediately apparent, people will take it as a secret they have found out about you. (In this context, it is interesting to note that in Latin America, where hairpieces are status symbols, the richest men are the ones who wear the most glaringly obvious toupees.) As the saying goes, if you have it, flaunt it. It's the one sure way to stop people from *whispering* that you have it.

Speaking of flaunting it, it was the "It" girl herself, Clara Bow, who set the model for dyeing one's hair with style. Not only did she dye hers a flaming red, she dyed the fur of her seven chow dogs the same color, and then made it a practice to drive around Hollywood with them in a bright red convertible. Now *that's* flaunting it.

But if flaunting is not your style, remember that you can never go wrong just leaving well enough alone. The history of Hollywood is replete with examples of film stars who went on to become famous for physical characteristics which their studio bosses originally wanted them to have "fixed." They wanted to paste back Clark Gable's ears; they wanted to put putty in the dimple in Kirk Douglas's chin; they wanted to put a wig and huge lashes on Bette Davis to make her look like Garbo. And in perhaps the most egregious example of all, they wanted Jane Fonda to have her jaw broken and reshaped, have her hair dyed blonde, and have her teeth reset. For good measure, they also advised her to wear falsies.

If that is not enough to make you think twice before overhauling your physical appearance, consider the experience of Gladys Deacon, the American beauty who dazzled English society earlier this century and later became Duchess of Marlborough. Although she was widely envied for her classically beautiful profile, she herself thought that it fell short of perfection, so to remedy the situation she had wax injected at the bridge of her nose. It worked—for a while. As the years passed the wax began to seep chinward, pushing her face out of shape as it moved, leaving behind a pathetically disfigured reminder of just how vengeful Mother Nature can be when you start meddling in her affairs.

TEST YOUR
STYLE QUOTIENT

1. If you are a stylist, and in possession of two adequately functioning legs, you will walk with a cane because:

    (a) You like canes.
    (b) You see yourself as a middle-aged dandy.
    (c) You are a born pessimist: You never know when you might suddenly be crippled.
    (d) You are a born-again pessimist: You never know when you might suddenly be attacked.

2. If you are a stylist, you will wear a mink coat with sneakers because:

    (a) You want to draw attention to your coat.
    (b) You want to draw attention to your feet.
    (c) You are always more comfortable in sneakers, and on this occasion you wish to be warm as well.
    (d) You stole the coat on the way here.

3. If you are a stylist, you will wear a hat indoors because:

    (a) You wish it to be known that you do not intend to stay long.
    (b) You wish it to be known that you do not distinguish between indoors and outdoors.
    (c) You never trusted roofs.
    (d) You are bald.

4. If you are a stylist, you will wear a flower in your button-hole because:

   (a) You are an undertaker.
   (b) You like flowers.
   (c) You like finding out which people have allergies.
   (d) You wish to appear old-fashioned.

5. If you are a stylist, you will take off your clothes in front of strangers because:

   (a) You want them to look at you with desire.
   (b) You want them to look at you with disgust.
   (c) You want them to look away.
   (d) It's hot in here.

(Answers on page 177)

SPEAKING

with Style

STYLE IN SPEECH IS SIMPLY
the ability to say exactly what you mean in a way that is distinctive. It is a skill that few possess.

Why this should be so is difficult to understand. The power of speech is the one thing that distinguishes us as a species, it is the trademark of our humanity, and as such it should be the one thing on which we expend the greatest effort and ingenuity. Moreover, it is something that is *given* to us: Unlike a large wardrobe, a large vocabulary costs nothing to assemble. Words are free. And they last forever. Also, whatever the language, speaking is an activity conducted according to rules—the words you use have fixed meanings, regardless of the different shadings and nuances they may be given in different contexts, and they follow one another in set patterns—so that anyone who takes the trouble to learn the rules immediately has at his disposal the most potent single force for the projection of his personality.

Clearly, then, the key to speaking with style is command of a vocabulary large enough to give you both flexibility and precision in expressing yourself. The more words you have, the more accurate and entertaining will be your self-portrayal in conversation. That much is obvious. What may be less obvious is that without the right words you will have a less interesting self to portray, because every word you are without is a thought or idea or concept you are without.

Likewise, every word about which you are confused is sooner or later going to create confusion about you. If you don't know the difference between *uninterested* and *disinterested, infer* and *imply, flaunt* and *flout, fortuitous* and *fortunate, climatic* and *climactic, subordinate* and *sublimate,* then how can you (or anyone else) ever be sure that you are saying what you really mean to say? Indeed, if you can't distinguish between the right word and the wrong word when there are dictionaries around to tell you which is which, how can you be trusted to know the difference between right and wrong in situations where there is no book to guide you?

But assuming that you have the words, and have them right, they will still not do the job for you unless you get them in the right order. That is why a strong sense of grammar is vital to the stylist. Grammar gives form to your speech, and if you can't form your speech properly, it is unlikely that you can give the proper form to your life, which is what style is all about. (It is, of course, possible to adopt a sort of premeditated formlessness as a style, in speaking as in life. Ezra Pound, for one, became a great poet by systematically breaking the rules of traditional English prosody. But he was only able to do it because he understood the rules in the first place.)

Failure to appreciate the importance of grammar has always been a handicap for the majority of the population. At any point in our history most people would probably have sympathized with the startled bemusement of Molière's Monsieur Jourdain in *Le Bourgeois Gentilhomme:* "Good Heavens! For more than forty years I have been speaking prose without knowing it." Nowadays, however, the teaching of grammar is so uniformly poor that you find most people speaking *bad* prose without knowing it. Such horrors as "between you and I," unheard (and unheard of) only a few years ago, have now become commonplace. Thus, at a time when our grammatical values have deteriorated so appallingly that we may soon find ourselves engulfed by mass incoherence, it is more important than ever for the stylist to maintain his own language in good working order.

Once you know the words and know how to put them together for maximum clarity, you will have fulfilled one of the two requirements for speaking with style: the ability to say exactly what you mean. The other requirement is the ability to say it *in a distinctive way*. This means, in general, that the more aphoristic your speech, the more epigrammatic, the better. Someone who has distilled his ideas and opinions into aphorisms, or at least into a form of commentary that is both concise and memorable, will always have a greater impact on his listeners than someone who does his thinking out loud.

Ironically, one of the ways of gauging that impact is by the amount of uneasiness your speech arouses. For reasons that have more to do with linguistic incompetence than with logic, most people are suspicious of sentiments that are elegantly or memorably phrased. They think that somehow you can't mean it. For these benighted souls, inarticulateness equals sincerity. In fact, of course, it is the other way around: "Smooth-talking" should be a compliment rather than a pejorative.

You will also be accused of repeating yourself (or at least you *should* be so accused), for someone who speaks with style will inevitably repeat himself. To begin with, there is no point in formulating a noteworthy observation on a given subject and then withholding it when the subject comes up. And if you are a stylist you can be certain that the same subjects *will* come up over and over again, because through your style you will have alerted the world to the subjects on which you are likely to have something distinctive to say.

Of course the final, crucial element in speaking with style is the delivery system itself: your voice. Here you have the perfect instrument for conveying your distinctiveness, for it is distinctive to begin with. No two voices are exactly alike —which is why law enforcement agencies now use "voice prints" as well as fingerprints as a means of identification. The challenge is to make your voice even more distinctive than it is already, so that one word from you over the telephone identifies you as unmistakably as would a glimpse of you in person.

There are two basic ways of doing this. The first, and easier, way is to capitalize on (and emphasize, even to the point of self-parody) the quirks, mannerisms, accent, and dialect that were bequeathed to you. The idea is to make your voice as revelatory of your style as it is of your background. This is the way chosen by a number of Hollywood's most illustrious film stars: James Cagney, John Wayne, Edward G. Robinson, James Stewart, and Humphrey Bogart (who wisely rejected advice to try to get rid of his lisp). It is no coincidence that these are also the actors who are the most often impersonated, nor that in each case the success of the impersonation depends almost entirely on getting the voice right.

The other way to make your voice more distinctive is to change it. This is a perfectly acceptable way, provided that your new voice—in its accent, timbre, cadence, and pronunciation—provides a more suitable soundtrack for the style you have chosen than the one you already have. This is what Tallulah Bankhead did when she traded in her backwoods Southern drawl for a mid-Atlantic voice. And it is what Clara Bow *should* have done before the talkies came in and revealed her to have a coarse Brooklyn accent, which quickly obliterated the image she had so carefully built up and caused her to fade from the screen soon thereafter.

Whichever way you choose to go, whether you emphasize your characteristic speech patterns or alter them, the purpose is the same: to make your voice so distinctive and recognizable that it becomes impossible for people to think of you without hearing it.

That said, we would now like to enumerate some of the subsidiary ways in which you can refine your style in speaking.

First of all: **Be consistent.** Just as you shouldn't have a different type of dress for different people or occasions, you shouldn't have a different manner of speaking. To the stylist, *all* speaking is public speaking, whether the audience consists of one thousand people or one.

Learn to listen. Some years ago the RAND Corporation in California conducted a study to try to determine why committees, even those composed of the most brilliant minds, were so notoriously bumbling and ineffective. Their conclusion: Nobody ever listens. Everyone on a committee is so eager to be heard himself that he doesn't bother to hear what the others are saying. The same, alas, is true of most conversations. In our eagerness to get our own message across, we often fail to hear what is actually being said to us. And thus we miss the opportunity to make a comment that is both pertinent and arresting. So remember that a good conversationalist is, first and foremost, a good listener. In fact, among people who are widely regarded as great conversationalists there are some who hardly ever open their mouths at all—which illustrates one of the bonuses of being a good listener: Because people have a tendency to remember the clever things they have said and to forget how they turned the conversation into a monologue, they are apt to give a large share of the credit for their own wit and wisdom to the one who simply listened to it.

Pause before speaking. This is not merely a rephrasing of the standard advice to think before you speak (although that is certainly sound advice). The point here is that you should be *seen* to be thinking before you speak, and therefore to be taking seriously what has been said to you. Even the shortest pause will add to your credentials as a good listener. Moreover, while you are using the extra seconds to sharpen (or perhaps edit) what you have to say, the brief silence preceding it will serve to heighten its effect.

Speak softly. Actually, there is nothing wrong with speaking loudly; it's just that you should always speak with more or less the same voice level, and since there are times when a loud voice is inappropriate, and no times when a soft voice is inappropriate, it is easier to keep your speaking voice style intact if you keep your voice down. Also, the higher the decibel count, the narrower the vocal range available to you for subtly stressing points you may wish to make. Finally, a soft voice commands closer attention than does a loud voice. People will hang on your every word only if they have to in order to *catch* every word. This is something that Mafia dons have long known, and that Muhammad Ali has recently learned.

Speak formally. As with the recommendation to speak softly, this suggestion is based on the need for consistency and flexibility. Since a stylist deals with everyone on the same level, and since there are times when informality is improper, if not impertinent, it is better to remain formal in speaking to people. Secondly, familiarity (especially when unsolicited) leaves you very little room to maneuver should you wish to change the character of a relationship: Any move to put greater distance between you and another person will be seen as a retreat into aloofness, and any movement in the other direction will be seen as a plunge toward intimacy. By maintaining a certain formality in addressing others, however, you can shift them around in your hierarchy of affections without compromising your style. And you will never be mistaken for an insurance salesman.

Speak the truth. Cecil Beaton once said, "Perhaps the world's second worst crime is boredom; the first is being a bore." Which is one reason why you should always tell the truth about yourself, because there is no one as boring as a liar. Another reason is that lying is a colossal waste of time—time spent keeping your stories straight (or identically bent), time spent remembering to whom you told what, and so on. But the best reason for telling the truth is that to lie is to signal that you are hiding something, and someone with style has nothing to hide. The only time a stylist ever lies is when the lie is so obvious and outrageous that the intent is clearly to entertain rather than to deceive. Frank Harris, whose *My Life and Loves* stands as a monument to this sort of lying, built an entire style around the baroque falsehood. As *The New Yorker* said of him, "He was a man with a gift for lying so marked as to amount to genius; even when the truth would serve him better, he preferred to introduce some spellbinding whopper, as more appropriate to his exceptional nature." Still, there is one major problem with this type of lying. It is the same problem that confronted the little boy who cried "Wolf!": People won't believe you when you're telling the truth. The burden of proof will always be on you. It is a burden no true stylist would ever willingly assume.

Don't try to be funny. Without a doubt, a sense of humor is a great blessing. In fact, it is arguable whether you can have style and *not* have a sense of humor. But that doesn't mean you should try to be funny. Somerset Maugham once observed that if you make people laugh they will think you trivial. While that isn't strictly true, he had a point: The *effort* to make people laugh is certainly trivializing. And when it involves the telling of jokes it is especially unfortunate, for jokes only breed other jokes, driving out genuine wit and humor from the conversation. Real humor has nothing to do with jokes, or with any other prefabricated narrative form. Real humor comes from the ability to see a situation from more than one point of view, and to describe or define it in terms of that perspective, often using language that is imported from an entirely different area of experience. It arises spontaneously in the course of conversation, and the laughter it provokes is likewise spontaneous, not sought after.

Avoid obscenity. Resorting to obscene language is a bad idea for three reasons. In the first place, it is distracting. It draws the listener's attention away from whatever else you have to say. In the second place, it is insulting to many people. It repels people whom you might otherwise attract. And in the third place it is almost always imprecise. With rare exceptions, an obscene word is nothing more than a crude substitute for a better word. However, as with lying, there are some people who can get away with obscenity by employing it on a grand scale. Hunter Thompson, the creator of "gonzo" journalism, is one of these. But unless, like Thompson, you think you have to be obscene to be believed, it is best to derive your imagery from sources other than bodily plumbing.

Avoid euphemisms. It is just as silly to be unnecessarily delicate as it is to be unnecessarily indelicate. People will always peel back the fig leaf to see what you are really saying, and they will wonder why you couldn't come out with it. Everyone knows that "senior citizens" are old people, that "job actions" are strikes, that "perspiration" is sweat, so why not say so? Why leave it up to your listeners to make their own translations? Euphemisms, like obscenities, call attention to themselves rather than to the sense of what you are saying. However, precisely because they *are* silly intrusions into your conversation, they can occasionally be used to good effect provided that they are pushed to the extremes of silliness. Thus, while it is fatuous to try to sanitize a bloody war by calling it a "conflict," it may be amusing to refer to it as an "unfortunate incident." Damon Runyon has a line in one of his stories which demonstrates this technique splendidly. It tells of the gruesome fate of a man who has been murdered —not by his enemies, but by "parties who do not wish him well." Euphemisms, then, do have a limited place in your repertoire, but only if they are sufficiently ludicrous to be entertaining.

Don't use more words than you need. Brevity is not just the soul of wit; it lies at the heart of all effective communication. The surest way to indicate that you have little or nothing to say is to say it at length. The weather, for example, is a topic about which very little of interest can be said. Consequently, most weather forecasters try to obscure the fact by adopting the most complicated way of saying the simplest thing: The chance of rain becomes "precipitation probability," rain itself becomes "shower activity," cold is attributed to the "wind-chill factor," and so on. Too, verbiage is frequently a sign that you don't know what you're talking about. To speak of "viable options," for instance, is to give evidence of seriously muddled thinking. An option is *by definition* viable; if it's not viable, it's not an option. The fewer words you use, then, the less risk there is that your speech will be infected by such redundancies. The way of concision is also the way to achieving greater impact for what you want to say. A splendid example that comes to mind occurs at the end of Nathanael West's novel, *Miss Lonelyhearts.* In the novel's climactic scene, the eponymous hero, a (male) newspaper columnist, is shot as he struggles with a man on a stairway. Now, a less skilled and less confident writer would have embellished this event by recording the columnist's demise in graphic, and probably sanguinary, detail. West, on the other hand, finished off his hero—and his book—with one simple, chilling sentence: "They both rolled part of the way down the stairs." *That's* style.

Avoid jargon and slang. Aesthetic considerations aside, both jargon and slang have two major drawbacks, either of which would be sufficient to disqualify them from having any place in the vocabulary of a stylist. The first is that they are both fashions, and someone with style doesn't follow fashions in speaking any more than in dressing. The second is that both are forms of groupspeak, and someone with style shuns identification with a group. In addition, both jargon and slang carry the handicap of imprecision. Slang words and phrases, most of which come nowadays from either the youthful counter-culture or the black subculture, as a rule embrace so many possible meanings as to be more confusing than clarifying. Someone who has been "ripped off," for example, may have been robbed, or burglarized, or defrauded, or cheated, or merely overcharged. But at least slang has the limited virtue of being vaguely meaningful, and often colorful, whereas jargon is almost always meaningless as well as colorless.

Currently, the two most virulent strains of jargon are those spawned by feminists and by technologists. The first group is responsible for such grotesque linguistic deformities as "chairperson," "waitperson," "anchorperson," and all the other "——persons." (It's a curious thing, as the English writer Brigid Brophy has pointed out, that no one in the Women's Lib movement seems to have realized that words such as "he" and "him," when not used to refer to a specific person, are metaphors rather than pronouns.) The second strain is the pseudo-scientific gibberish spread by the exhaust fans of High Tech. In low concentrations—the occasional "input" or "parameters" or "interface"—it is unpleasant but hardly lethal. In large doses, however, it becomes a blight that completely destroys the language. To see just how bad it can get, consider this gaseous emission from the mouth of a Boston television reporter who was sent to do a story on how the airlines would fare with large numbers of people staying home over Christmas. His report consisted of a solemn discourse on "how the no-show factor will impact on the airlines in a holiday situation." Sad to say, the man's tongue was not cut out on the spot.

Avoid certain subjects. To wit:

Personal disasters. Whether they show it or not, most people are profoundly indifferent to your pain and suffering, so to inflict on them the story of your accident, or illness, or operation, or breakdown, or divorce, or bereavement, or unemployment is to provoke resentment and in many cases retaliation (in the form of matching stories about *their* disasters). The only justification for introducing such subjects into a conversation is for purposes of entertainment, and then you must make it clear from the outset that your story is being offered for people's amusement and not for their sympathy. Even at that, the story should be condensed into a single anecdote or epigram. The best rule to follow is the one enunciated by W. H. Auden: "A suffering, a weakness, which cannot be expressed as an aphorism should not be mentioned."

Your sex life. Of course, for some people this topic will fall under the above category, but whether you count your sexual experiences among your triumphs or your disasters, you should always refrain from discussing them. Self-congratulation is as boring as self-pity. And, as with self-pity, it invites reciprocity, thus raising the alarming prospect of having to listen to tales of someone *else's* sexual exploits. In any case, remember that there is no story you can possibly tell about your sex life from which you emerge with style.

Your past. Obviously, to banish all talk of your past from your conversation would be impossible—and impoverishing. Anything that has enriched your life should be allowed to enrich your conversation. What should be avoided are prolonged excursions into oral autobiography. Of all the ways of killing a conversation, perhaps the most painful is death by reminiscence.

The flaws of others. In one way or another, everything you say against others will sooner or later be used against you. Therefore, to quote everybody's mother, if you can't say something nice about someone, it's best not to say anything at all. This doesn't mean that you can't describe the flawed behavior of others; it only means that you shouldn't identify it as such. Leave it to others to decide whether the behavior is blameworthy or not.

Any subject on which your opinion is too eagerly solic-

ited. Whenever people are a little *too* anxious to know what you think about a given subject, the chances are that they simply want an excuse to give you *their* opinion. In other words, they are looking for either an endorsement or an argument. To avoid being put in the position of having to provide either, there are several types of evasive action you can take. One is the flat declaration of ignorance: You don't know anything about the subject. Another is a declaration of neutrality: You make it a practice not to have an opinion on the subject. Alternatively, you can offer a theory so preposterous that you effectively disqualify yourself from speaking on the subject. But undoubtedly the best way for the stylist is to single out something, anything, about the subject for which you can profess admiration. And, where possible, that something should be thoroughly inconsequential, because then it will also be uncontroversial. Ronald Firbank, the English author, demonstrated his mastery of this technique on one notable occasion when a fellow author doggedly tried to get a literary opinion out of him. Firbank at last responded, sweetly: "I adore italics, don't you?" Firbank had style.

TEST YOUR
STYLE QUOTIENT

1. If you are a stylist, you will whisper because:

   (a) You wish to go unnoticed.
   (b) You wish to be noticed.
   (c) You have a sore throat.
   (d) You are dying.

2. If you are a stylist, you will frequently employ foreign phrases in your conversation because:

   (a) You have a proper concern for *le mot juste*.
   (b) You want to display your cosmopolitanism.
   (c) You want to parody those who want to display their cosmopolitanism.
   (d) You have run off with the *au pair*.

3. If you are a stylist, you will fail to answer questions because:

   (a) You are hard of hearing.
   (b) You know that anything you say may be taken down and used against you.
   (c) You don't know the answer.
   (d) You know the answer, but you despise the question.

4. If you are a stylist, you will often resort to clichés because:

   (a) You want to be understood by the multitudes.
   (b) You want to be left alone.
   (c) You want to ridicule the use of clichés.
   (d) You want to ridicule yourself.

5. If you are a stylist, you will occasionally find it helpful to use an accent other than your own because:

   (a) You want to upgrade your status in order to impress.
   (b) You want to downgrade your status in order to amuse.
   (c) You want to make an editorial comment.
   (d) You miss Peter Sellers.

(Answers on page 178)

EATING
AND DRINKING

with Style

THERE IS NOTHING WHICH HAS yet been contrived by man by which so much happiness is produced as by a good tavern or inn." So declared Samuel Johnson over two centuries ago, and among people with style his sentiments still find an enthusiastic echo today. Indeed, for anyone who appreciates good food, good wine, and good company, there is no place on earth more sacred than one's favorite restaurant.

At the same time, for those who are uncertain about the rituals of dining out, a good restaurant has more booby traps than a minefield. It can be a torture chamber for the insecure.

Of course, any place can be a torture chamber for the insecure. The reason that a restaurant holds more terrors than most is that it is a small, closed society—rigidly structured, hierarchical, with its own set of laws and customs. In such a setting no false move goes unnoticed, and thus every move carries with it the risk of humiliation.

In a moment we will consider the protocol that governs restaurant behavior, but first we would like to say a word about restaurants in general. If eating out often is part of your style, it is a good idea to choose one restaurant as a regular (and permanent) nesting place. It is difficult to be the central figure in your own landscape—which is the aim of any stylist—if the scenery is constantly changing. Dr. Johnson, for one, appreciated this. Over the years he sat at the same table in the same pub until it became a virtual pulpit for the propagation of his opinions.

Apart from the one overriding advantage of providing you with a consistent backdrop, there are other advantages to patronizing one restaurant exclusively. First of all, it provides comfortable and familiar surroundings in which to entertain should you prefer not to entertain at home. Secondly, it enhances both your visibility and availability: People will always know where they can find you. In addition, assuming that the chosen restaurateur is properly grateful for your custom, you can use the restaurant both as a bank and an answering service, to cash checks and to pick up messages. And, of course, in those times when you find yourself a little short on cash, it's good to know that there is one place where you can eat now and pay later.

In choosing the restaurant that will be your home away from home, it is important, obviously, to pick the one that best suits your style. It may be a sidewalk cafe or a dimly lit sepulcher, a temple of *haute cuisine* or a crowded cafeteria; it may be large or small, noisy or quiet. It doesn't matter whether there is sawdust on the floor or chandeliers on the ceiling, so long as the ambience is appropriate to your style.

As in the selection of everything else, when deciding on a restaurant you should avoid the fashionable—unless, that is, the perfect restaurant for you also happens to be one that is in vogue at the moment. And even then you run the risk of having your identity overwhelmed by the identity of the place itself. Nor are fashionable places particularly hospitable to the newcomer. Wherever fragile egos congregate to demonstrate their acceptance by the "In" crowd, they tend to protect their territory from invaders with special ferocity. As the restaurant critic of *New York* magazine once wrote of Elaine's, the famous celebrity hangout on Manhattan's Upper East Side, "the crowd, the waiters, and Elaine herself are old hands at smelling blood."

Once you have established yourself as an habitué of a particular restaurant, you can do your guests and yourself a favor by always recommending to them dishes that you know to be good. This saves them the problem of choosing blind from an unfamiliar menu (and thus saves the time wasted in indecision), and it saves you unnecessary expense by subtly giving them an indication of what you can afford. By the same token, whenever you are someone else's guest at a meal it is a good practice to ask for—and, if possible, follow—the recommendation of your host.

Surprisingly, there are still quite a few people who look upon a strange menu as if it were an examination paper, something placed in front of them to test their knowledge and sophistication rather than to convey information. If you are a stylist, you will never permit yourself any such anxieties. Whenever you find yourself confronted with dishes or names of dishes which are unfamiliar to you, you shouldn't hesitate to ask for an explanation or a translation. Make a point, or even a joke, of your ignorance. Never try to hide it. And if you subsequently decide that your taste runs to simpler fare than that found on the menu, don't be afraid to admit it. It only shows that you know what you like, and it gives the restaurant an opportunity to sell less elaborately prepared food for the same price.

Roughly the same rules apply to the ordering of wine. Don't pretend that you know (or care) more about it than you actually do. If it is your job to select the wine, and it is a job for which you are unqualified either by reason of ignorance or indifference, proclaim that fact and pass on the job to someone else (including the waiter, if no one else volunteers). Later, when the wine arrives at your table, you will probably be asked to participate in two further decisions, one of which is pointless and the other generally misunderstood. As to the first, the question of whether to let the wine "breathe" for a while, it doesn't matter what you decide because wine *can't* breathe while it's still in the bottle. That is, not enough of it is exposed to the air to make any appreciable difference to the taste.

The second decision, whether or not to taste the wine before it is served, is somewhat trickier. Most people, it seems, have the mistaken notice that the ritual sip of wine which the waiter offers is either a *pro forma* gesture or an opportunity to decide if you like the wine you have ordered. It is neither. It's *assumed* that you like the wine or you wouldn't have ordered it; the point of tasting it is simply to ensure that this particular bottle is in good condition. In other words, you take a sip of the wine because you already *know* what it tastes like, not because you want to find out. Therefore it's silly, if not dishonest, to go through the solemn business of tasting a wine if you don't have any idea what it's *supposed* to taste like. Here again the best course is to embrace your limitations by foregoing the ritual tasting or by passing it on to someone else.

On the other hand, assuming that you *are* qualified to judge the merits of a given bottle of wine, you must be prepared to send it back if it is below standard. Indeed, you should be prepared to send it back even if you are *not* so qualified. Otherwise why go to the bother of tasting it first? Now, most people tremble at this suggestion. They would rather drink kerosene than risk ruining an occasion by having a confrontation with a waiter, especially if that confrontation is likely to expose their ignorance. But there are ways of handling this situation with style, and without unpleasantness. The secret, in a word, is humility. Whether you are quite certain that the bottle you have been served is of inferior quality, or whether you merely suspect that something might be wrong with it, you should leave the final judgment up to others. First ask for your companions to be given a taste. If that fails to produce a clear verdict, ask the wine waiter to taste the wine himself. If that, too, leaves the fate of the wine undecided, ask that the proprietor be given a taste. Almost any proprietor, even if he disagrees with your judgment, will take his cue from this and offer to substitute another bottle of wine. A good restaurateur is more interested in saving *your* face than his own.

It should be noted, incidentally, that with the final ordering of the food and drink the two subjects should cease to exist as topics of conversation. Nothing is more tedious than a running commentary on whatever it is that you happen to be doing at a particular moment, especially if it is something that everyone has to do in order to survive, such as eating and drinking. Food and drink are to be consumed, not dwelt upon.

The person with style will also take care to be gracious to the waiters, however slow or forgetful they may be. It is both styleless and contemptible to take advantage of the fact that someone is serving you by reminding him that he is your servant. Anyone who thinks he has to be aggressive or peremptory to get good service betrays an abject lack of confidence in his *right* to get good service.

Also on the subject of the treatment of waiters, the matter of tipping is worth a mention. Like most personal gestures involving money, tipping is a frequent cause of embarrassment. It shouldn't be. A tip is simply a fee for a job, with the going rate fixed by custom. While you can adjust the fee slightly upward or downward in accordance with your opinion of the service rendered, you should never go too far in either direction except in cases of exceptionally good (or exceptionally bad) service. Overtipping, the classic faux pas of the parvenu, will be seen either as compensation for one's boorish conduct or as a bribe for special treatment in the future. Undertipping will be seen as an expression of either stinginess or revenge. A stylist would not wish to be associated with any of these motives. In any event, a tip is an ineffectual form of either reward or punishment, because in most good restaurants the tips all go into one pot to be distributed later among the staff. If you want to make an effective comment on the quality of the restaurant, the best reward you have to offer is your stylish presence, the worst punishment your absence.

On the question of table manners, the first thing that ought to be said is that good manners do not a stylist make. Even the most devout observance of the conventions of etiquette will not confer style on someone who lacks it to begin with. On the other hand, poor manners can certainly *un*make a stylist. Indeed, there was once a time in Japan when a man could be executed for exhibiting poor table manners.

If this seems somewhat excessive, it does show an awareness of the true function of manners: to show respect for the feelings of others, to avoid causing them discomfort. Good manners are not a semaphore of good breeding, a kind of code developed to signify social rank; rather, they are simply a means of not offending the sensibilities of others. In the context of the dining table, what this comes down to is the art of satisfying your appetite without ruining the appetite of somebody else.

It is an art that Americans have had some difficulty in mastering. As long ago as 1853, William Makepeace Thackeray, the author of *Vanity Fair,* wrote to an American friend: "The European continent swarms with your people. They are not all as polished as Chesterfield. . . . I saw five of them at supper at Basle the other night with their knives down their throats. It was awful." And as recently as 1979, Walter Hoving, then chairman of Tiffany's, appeared on the "Today" show to demonstrate for the television audience the most elementary table manners, such as how to hold your knife and fork without looking as if you're expecting to be suddenly attacked by a street gang.

What is so puzzling about all this is that it takes no more effort to eat decorously than it does to eat like a garbage compactor. No special knowledge or training is required, and the actual skills involved are minimal. To resist acquiring these skills, therefore, is almost an act of aggression. At best, it reveals an anti-social attitude that is incompatible with style.

Much the same can be said for excessive drinking. It indicates a willful abandonment of control, and thus a willingness to bore people or otherwise make them feel uncomfortable. In fact, so painful is the company of a drunk that it almost justifies drinking in self-defense. As the great humorist George Jean Nathan once confessed, "I drink to make other people interesting."

Once again, then, the point of good manners—at the dining table and elsewhere—is not to show how dignified you can be, but to acknowledge the dignity of others. In short, good manners are a way of paying others a compliment.

Perhaps the ultimate example of good table manners occurred at a dinner party given by Count Boni de Castellane in France shortly before World War I. Among the guests was an elderly French lady who suddenly became ill toward the end of the meal. Suspecting that she was about to die, she discreetly summoned a waiter and whispered to him to bring the dessert as quickly as possible. It was not that she wanted to go out on a full stomach; it was just that she wanted to make sure that the party had risen from the table before she expired. Her sole concern was that the other guests should not be discomfited by the sight of her dropping dead at the table. A short while later, when the meal was over, she died. With style.

TEST YOUR STYLE QUOTIENT

1. If you are a stylist, you will eat with your hands because:

   (a) You wish to call attention to the fact that you were not provided with cutlery.
   (b) You wish to remind people that you are a cultural anthropologist.
   (c) You wish to express your contempt for etiquette.
   (d) You are an animal.

2. If you are a stylist, you will ask for a second helping because:

   (a) You liked the first one.
   (b) You are still hungry.
   (c) You wish to pay your host a compliment.
   (d) You are known for your gluttony.

3. If you are a stylist, you will decline to eat the food that is served because:

   (a) You are not hungry.
   (b) You are dieting.
   (c) You do not like what is on the plate.
   (d) Your appetite is for spiritual things.

4. If you are a stylist, you will find it necessary to become intoxicated because:

   (a) You want to forgive.
   (b) You want to forget.
   (c) You want to show your contempt for the deadly sobriety all around you.
   (d) You can't get too much of a good thing.

5. If you are a stylist, you will request a doggie bag in a restaurant because:

   (a) You have a doggie.
   (b) You are thinking of the starving millions in Africa.
   (c) You are thinking of the one who has to wash the dishes.
   (d) You want to know where your next meal is coming from.

(Answers on page 178)

MATING AND MARRYING

with Style

I N HIS MEMOIR, *The Thirties,*
Edmund Wilson confessed at one point to having uncharac-
teristic difficulty with the language. "It is certainly very
hard," he wrote, "to write about sex in English without
making it unattractive."

This is undoubtedly true, but it is still an odd remark
for a writer of Wilson's stature, for it seems to imply that the
fault lies with English rather than with the subject. The fact
is that it is difficult to make sex attractive in *any* language,
for the simple reason that sex itself is unattractive. Look at
pornography, which is the graphic depiction of sex in its
purest, or rawest, form: It may be compelling, or arousing,
or amusing, or all of these—but it is not pretty. If anything,
sex and beauty are at odds with one another, as Bette Davis
slyly acknowledged in one of her most memorable lines: "I'd
love to kiss you but I just washed my hair."

But its unattractiveness is just one of the problems sex
poses for the stylist. Another is that it is very difficult to be
naked with style. The sum is diminished by the sight of the
parts. Also, for sex—conventional sex, that is—you require a
partner, which makes it a group activity. And a stylist avoids
anything that requires membership of a group, even if it's a
group of only two. Nor does the sexual act itself allow much

scope for the expression of individuality, because in whatever version it's performed it is still predetermined by anatomy; it always comes down to the question of what goes where.

Moreover, whether you indulge in sex for pleasure or procreation, for gratification or relief, it remains a goal-oriented exercise. And stylists do not have goals other than the refinement of their style. There is, too, a competitive angle to sex nowadays that further reduces its appeal for the stylist. Ever since Freud discovered that sex was the real center of the universe, thereby unleashing hordes of "sexologists" to peer through our keyholes, we have been inundated with bulletins on each other's physical apparatus and the effectiveness of its employment. The result has been an epidemic of what is called performance anxiety, as people want to know how they rate as lovers compared with others. This in turn gives rise to jealousy—even retroactive jealousy—which only makes the competitive aspect more acute. Needless to say, this is not the sort of atmosphere in which style flourishes.

Furthermore, the desire for sex exposes you, both literally and figuratively, to situations constantly fraught with the possibility of rejection or humiliation. Unless your style is to be a victim—a Woody Allen type, for instance—these are not promising situations. (And even Woody Allen doesn't make a very convincing Woody Allen type. Although he casts himself in the role of the bumbling suitor, he always makes sure that he gets every pretty girl that he lusts after—a role confusion that may explain why he has spent so much time in psychoanalysis.)

Finally, sex carries the risk that your partner will later be seized by an uncontrollable urge to tell the world all about your couplings. Of course, you may react to such a prospect the way the Duke of Wellington did when his mistress threatened to publish her diary: "Publish and be damned!" But when one surveys the intimacies vouchsafed to us by such as Elizabeth Ray, Judith Exner, Britt Ekland, Anna Kashfi, Susan Strasberg, Shelley Winters, Margaret Trudeau et al., one is forced to conclude that your style would be better served if you use your bed exclusively for sleeping.

Then again, you may be such a gifted sexual athlete that it is in your interest to have your erotic adventures made public. Indeed, one way to have sex with style is to make sex the *basis* of your style. This is what Errol Flynn did—so successfully, in fact, that his popularity *increased* when he was accused of statutory rape by two teenage girls, causing his name to enter the language as the epitome of sexual success: "In like Flynn." Likewise, the powerful industrialist Coleman du Pont is remembered not for his interest in the family chemical business but for his abiding interest in young women. (Once, entering a hotel suite, he found a pair of silk knickers behind the sofa, which he handed to the porter with the command, "Take these out and have them filled.") Sarah Bernhardt and Mae West are two more whose amorous escapades became legendary. But probably the supreme example of someone who made sex a style in itself was Marie Duplessis, the most expensive courtesan in Paris in the early nineteenth century. By the age of nineteen she had seven distinguished gentlemen lavishly supporting her, each of whom was allotted one night of the week. Regardless of their generosity or their eminence (Alexandre Dumas and Franz Liszt were among her lovers), if they wanted her favors they had to keep to *her* schedule.

There are, however, two problems with building your style around your sexuality. One is that you need to have a genuine talent for sex; mere competence is not enough. As Ezra Pound once remarked, he saw nothing wrong with people of mediocre ability playing the piano, it was the giving of concerts that he objected to. The other problem is that, like your looks, your sexual prowess is bound to fade with age. Which means that you will end up either being forced to preside over the decline of your style, or being forced to change it altogether. Neither is a very happy prospect.

The Victorians, for all their hypocrisy in the matter of sex, understood very well the relationship between sex and style. That is, they understood that the two should either be kept as far apart as possible or be completely interwoven. Thus for Victorian women sex was either an ordeal to be endured or a career to be pursued, while for Victorian men it was either a necessary chore to produce offspring or a bawdy delight to be purchased from a professional.

Today, however, the amateurs have taken over sex. No longer is guilt the "existential edge of sex," as Norman Mailer would like it to be; what flavor it has now comes from technique. What once was either a mysterious and sanctifying union or a mortal sin is now a hobby for the masses, complete with manuals, accessories, specialist shops, and even clubs for the really dedicated hobbyists. So it is no wonder that sex has little place in style. Style is a serious business, not a hobby.

There is one way, however, to expand the place of sex in style, and that is by reintroducing the now-defunct notion of romance. In other words, it is the *process,* not the consummation, that gives style to an intimate encounter. It is what *leads up to* sex, rather than the sex itself, that determines the degree of style connected with any liaison. To appreciate this, you need look no further than the example of Casanova, the greatest lover of them all. Apart from being a distinguished soldier, philosopher, musician, author, businessman, diplomat, gastronome, and raconteur, he was a man of infinite charm and romance—and *that* is what accounted for his success as a lover. Similarly, it was the charm and courtliness of Porfirio Rubirosa, the last of the great playboys, which made him so attractive to some of the world's richest and most beautiful women. They were attracted to him not because he was "good in bed," but because he was good everywhere else.

The most stylish liaisons, then, will be those in which the romantic element far outweighs the sexual element. Indeed, while it is impossible to have too much romance in a close relationship, it is possible to have the most passionate and loving relationship with no sex at all. It is even possible to have such a relationship, with style, without the physical presence of the other person. George Bernard Shaw used to contend that the perfect love affair was one "conducted entirely by post," and he followed his own maxim by conducting a long and ardent correspondence with the actress Ellen Terry. Likewise, Flaubert's one serious affair was restricted almost exclusively to a long exchange of letters. And Maxwell Perkins, the great editor of Hemingway and Fitzgerald, expressed his fervent devotion to Elizabeth Lemmon, a Virginia lady, solely by correspondence. For a quarter of a century they carried on a passionate affair while remaining celibate.

To most people, raised on the notion that sex is central to one's well-being, affairs such as these will seem strange and unfulfilling. Even Dr. Johnson, who understood almost everything, would have had trouble understanding them. He once wrote: "Marriage has many pains, but celibacy has no pleasures." That may be so, but it is a mistake to think that pleasure, which is only temporarily satisfying, is the same thing as happiness, which is permanently rewarding. It is mistaken also to think that pleasure necessarily leads to happiness. As often as not, pleasure—especially carnal pleasure—leads to desires and expectations which cannot be satisfied, and therefore leads to unhappiness rather than happiness.

On the other hand, Dr. Johnson was certainly right

about the pains of marriage. Not only are they numerous, but, unlike the pleasures, they tend to endure and intensify. That being the case, it is difficult to comprehend why we as a species have this seemingly overpowering urge to pair off with one another.

It is harder still to understand why we do it the *way* we do it—by means of an oral contract ratified by the state (and, often, the church). Moreover, it is a uniquely binding contract in that, unlike any other legal agreement, it cannot be abrogated by mutual consent of the parties involved; state intervention is required to terminate it. And this in spite of the fact that the marriage covenant is based on the most irrational of premises. Shaw summed it up nicely: "When two people are under the influence of the most violent, most insane, most delusive, and most transient of passions, they are required to swear that they will remain in that excited, abnormal, and exhausting condition until death do them part."

But it would be pointless to dwell on the basic absurdity of the marriage vows, because the real risks lie in the unforeseen aspects of the condition that the vows formalize. Put simply, which is how Sir Francis Bacon put it in his treatise, *Of Marriage and Single Life,* spouses are "impediments to great enterprises." And there is no greater enterprise than the perfecting of one's style.

The first problem with marriage, for the stylist, is that it disturbs your concentration on yourself and at the same time blurs your focus on others. Just as a camera cannot focus on both the foreground and the background simultaneously, it is difficult for even the greatest of stylists to project their personalities both near and far without a loss of sharpness. Secondly, the stylist who marries runs the risk of a loss of consistency. It is almost unavoidable that two people who live together will develop their own private code, in actions as well as words, which invariably leads to a division between

Them and Us. A stylist wants less distance, not more, between himself and the rest of the world.

Another problem with being a marriage partner is that, as a member of a team, there is enormous pressure on you to make behavioral compromises, to suppress your individuality, for the benefit of the team. Worse, the pressure is seldom obvious or direct; it works subtly and cumulatively, until one day you find that you have unconsciously adopted many of the gestures, mannerisms, and even attitudes of your mate. (Hence the phenomenon of old couples who have come to look and sound like each other.) You cannot be yourself—and thus you cannot be a stylist—when you are also being someone else.

Finally, and paradoxically, the "better" the marriage, the more circumscribed will be your contacts and experiences outside the marriage. Even if you don't succumb to the temptation to shut the door on the outside world and let your mate stand as proxy for all those who are excluded from your attention, the world itself will close many doors on you. The first thing people will consider is not your singularity but the fact that you are coupled to someone else; thus you will be cut off from all those situations in which the presence of a couple might be awkward or inappropriate. This is especially true, as we noted, of couples whose devotion to each other is all-surpassing. Walter Lippmann, of all people, said it best when he wrote that "lovers who have nothing to do but love each other are not really to be envied; love and nothing else very soon is nothing else."

To obviate some of the more stifling restrictions imposed by wedlock, more and more people today are turning to variations on the theme of marriage in the mistaken belief that you can get around the disadvantages of a partnership simply by toying with the form that partnership takes. Thus you have the Quasi-Marriage, two people living together under the illusion that their unmarried status confers a significant measure of independence. And you have the New Marriage, in which the two partners draw up a marriage contract on the ludicrous assumption that the principal issues involved in matrimony can be spelled out in a document. Then there is what might be called Marriage Plus, in which extramarital affairs are built into the arrangement, thereby making the arrangement itself somewhat redundant. And lastly there is the Anti-Marriage, popularized by the rebellious youth of the sixties, in which the partners strenuously flout all the conventions of marriage—an exercise as joyless as it is pointless.

These are all in their various ways as restrictive and irrational as the traditional form of marriage which they are intended to replace. Far from dealing with the central problem with marriage—the fact that it is a joint venture—they merely obscure it by introducing a new set of problems. So if you cannot resist the urge to bind yourself to someone, at least do it properly, legally. Better, do it triumphantly; invite the world to your wedding.

However, if your marriage is not to get in the way of your style, you must be exceedingly careful in selecting your mate. To begin with, your future partner must be someone who completely accepts your view of yourself. Never, never get involved with someone who wants to change you. If you have style, any change can only be for the worse.

Secondly, your mate should be of approximately the same age and background. Anyone who forges a marital alliance across generational, racial, or class boundaries invites the sort of attention (and suspicion) that distracts from one's style. When Gloria Vanderbilt at twenty-one married the sixty-three-year-old Leopold Stokowski, for example, or when Princess Caroline of Monaco went slumming to the altar with Philippe Junot, the world's attention quickly shifted away from the styles of the parties involved to unflattering speculation concerning their motives for contracting such clearly doomed marriages. Similarly, Nancy Cunard's commitment to civil rights for blacks, Peggy Guggenheim's devotion to modern art, and Jane Fonda's conversion to political activism were all greeted with widespread skepticism because of the strong suspicion in each case that the cause adopted was nothing more than the offspring of an unlikely liaison.

Thirdly, in selecting a mate you should go for someone who will reinforce your strengths rather than compensate for your weaknesses. Remember that your limitations are as much a part of your style as your abilities, and thus if you marry someone who will make up for what you lack you will almost certainly end up with your style being whittled away in the name of self-improvement. The best partner for a stylist, then, is someone who will bring to the marriage not something that you are missing but more of what you already have.

Obviously, as the whole raison d'être of marriage is its permanence, you should only consider as a prospective marriage partner someone whose appeal is likely to endure. Because of all the ways of correcting a mistake, divorce is undoubtedly the messiest. Nonetheless, the world being the way it is, one must take into account the fact that even marriages apparently made in heaven can turn hellish. As the sage Duc de la Rochefoucauld observed, "If one judges love by the majority of its effects, it is more like hatred than like friendship." So it is only realistic to include in our discussion a brief mention of the way to *end* a marriage with style.

Ideally, a marriage should end the way it began—with rejoicing and the promise of great things to come. Divorce should not be confused with defeat, nor should it be treated as an occasion for inventorying What Went Wrong. And of course it should not be accompanied by demeaning squabbles over who gets which property. (*Nothing* should be accompanied by squabbles over property.) Above all, something as pure as divorce should never be sullied by financial considerations. To ask for alimony is to ask for a delayed paycheck, and thus to admit that the marriage was simply a form of employment. Or it is asking for war reparations, which is to admit that the marriage was a form of combat. Either way it is utterly styleless.

But enough about divorce. It is something to be considered only after the style has gone out of a marriage, and we are concerned here with how to put style *into* a marriage. To this end it is instructive to look at some of the more spectacular examples of people who have been married with style: Henry II and Eleanor of Aquitaine, Franklin and Eleanor Roosevelt, Juan and Eva Peron, Alfred Lunt and Lynn Fontanne, Richard Burton and Elizabeth Taylor. The first thing one notices about these marriages is that they were truly ensemble performances; each partner in them played a role that always reminded one of the existence of the other partner. They also had a certain inevitability about them. As a friend remarked when Orson Welles and Rita Hayworth were married, "Where else could they go?" And, finally, there was a kind of divine symmetry about them which, as Juan Peron and the Burtons later demonstrated, could not be duplicated in other partnerships.

Nowhere can these characteristics be better seen than in the marriage of the Duke and Duchess of Windsor. By any standard, except the accidental one of birthright, these were two extremely marginal people, yet when they came together they created a kingdom over which they ruled for the better part of four decades. Their style, quite simply, was one another—and they carried it off to such perfection that their union remains the supreme example of being married with style.

It should be noted, however, that their style was achieved only at the cost of submerging their individual identities in their corporate identity. That is a devastatingly high price to pay. So unless you are persuaded that you are one of those rare people whose personality is best expressed in the context of someone else's personality, it is better not to put your style at the service of your marriage, but to put your marriage at the service of your style.

In other words, make married life an audition for real life.

TEST YOUR
STYLE QUOTIENT

1. If you are a stylist, you will allow yourself to be sexually aroused because:

   (a) You have been celibate too long.
   (b) You have met a true sexual stylist.
   (c) You have satyriasis.
   (d) Arousal is such a persuasive form of flattery.

2. If you are a stylist, you will find it acceptable to discuss your sex life because:

   (a) You want to encourage others to talk about theirs.
   (b) You want to seduce somebody.
   (c) You want to poke fun at sex itself.
   (d) You want to put a stop to another conversation already in progress.

3. If you are a stylist, you will marry very young because:

    (*a*) You want to satisfy your lustful curiosity.
    (*b*) You want to get away from home.
    (*c*) You want to annoy your older sister.
    (*d*) You want someone to share the rent.

4. If you are a stylist, you will marry very late because:

    (*a*) You want to have the experience just once.
    (*b*) You want to quell rumors of your sexual deviation.
    (*c*) It takes a long time to find the right person.
    (*d*) Your new spouse is both rich and generous.

5. If you are a stylist, you will marry very often because:

    (*a*) You are trying to get it right.
    (*b*) You are trying to get in the papers.
    (*c*) You are trying to get even with your ex-spouses.
    (*d*) You are trying to get presents.

(*Answers on page 178*)

CREATING
A HOME

with Style

T HERE ARE A NUMBER OF different ways of viewing the place where you live. One is to see your home as your castle, your private domain where you are sovereign regardless of your position in the outside world. Another is to see it in purely functional terms, as the great architect Le Corbusier did when he defined a house as simply "a machine for living in." Or you might see it as nothing more than the last stop on the line—a place, in Barbara Stanwyck's words, "where you go when you run out of places."

If you are a stylist, however, you will see your home as another medium for your message: something that you put around you, like your clothes, in order to tell people who you are.

Generally speaking, when you come to decide on a place to live it is best to locate in the midst of a large city. The reason should be obvious: There you find the greatest number, and the greatest variety, of people. And people are to the stylist what water is to the swimmer. In addition, the relationships you form in a city are less confining than they are in a smaller community, where every misunderstanding tends to have a ripple effect. And, of course, there are more things to *do* in a big city. Hence the opportunities are greater for the exercise of your style.

This is not to say that stylists are to be found only in the great metropolitan centers. You can live anywhere with style—in a cabin in the woods, in a slum in a ghetto, even in Beverly Hills. But it is *easiest* to live with style where you are constantly exposed to many different kinds of people and experience. That is why it is probably hardest to be a stylist in the suburbs: It's a struggle just to keep from being suffocated by all that dreary sameness.

Needless to say, there is no such thing as a "good address" or a "bad address" where style is concerned. Style does not reside in any particular part of town. At the same time, it is also true that stylists tend to avoid areas where all the Streets have been promoted to Drives in an attempt to give them a little more class. The example of such an area that comes first to mind is Beverly Hills, where (so the joke goes) the bums and winos live on Skid Drive.

Another reason for choosing carefully the place you intend to live is that it will be your permanent base. Not that you will never move again: On the contrary, it is probable that the time will come when moving will be a good idea, if not a necessity. The point is that, unless circumstances dictate otherwise, you should avoid moving with any frequency. Bear in mind that your home is not only the staging area for your style, it is also your stage. So if you want to maintain the visibility and predictability that are two of the hallmarks of the true stylist, you can't afford to present a constantly moving target.

Furthermore, an inability to stay for long in the same place indicates that you are having trouble deciding where you belong—that is to say, trouble deciding who you are. The same is true of people who feel the need for a dual home base. Thus when Gore Vidal decided to divide his residence between Rome and Hollywood (a rather startling contrast, to say the least) it made his admirers wonder which represents the real Vidal.

Once you have settled on your place of residence, there is the question of how to furnish and decorate it. This is a crucial matter because it involves the immediate setting, the backdrop, for your style. To quote the English art critic Edward Lucie-Smith, the colors and objects with which we surround ourselves form the "scenery for a play which we make up as we go along."

Remember that your domestic interior is the only part of your environment over which you have total control, and therefore it represents, and will be seen as, one of the definitive statements about your style.

In decorating your home, as in decorating your person, the first and only rule is to ignore fashion. Never choose things because they represent a look that is "in." You should choose things because they represent *you*. Similarly, never get rid of things just because *Better Homes & Gardens* has certified them to be outmoded, or because eyebrows have been raised at the sight of them. If you really see something of yourself in rattan furniture or pink flamingos, if you are really more comfortable with electric logs in the fireplace and blue water in the toilet, then there is no good reason to make a change. Only if the things around you are unsuitable as spokesmen for your style should you move to replace them.

Indeed, in that case, you should dispense with them immediately, whether or not they can be replaced. In any statement about your style (such as your living quarters) no contradictions can be tolerated, even if they were introduced into your presence by a well-heeled and well-meaning mother-in-law. However valuable or expensive something may be, unless it reflects your own personal taste it will distort the image of yourself that you want to project.

To create a home with style, you must be the collector—
not just the curator—of the things you live among.

And as with everything else that you incorporate into
your style, your domestic surroundings must tell the truth
about you. If you live in a place you only *wish* you could
afford, or if your walls are hung with pictures you think you
ought to like, or if your shelves are lined with books you
some day *hope* to read, these little lies will catch up with
you sooner or later.

By the same token, if your taste is more richly endowed
than your wallet, it is a mistake to settle for imperfect repre-
sentations of that taste. Never surround yourself with second
choices. If you can only afford your first choice in a few items,
it is better to let those few stand as isolated metaphors for
your taste than to scramble the message with symbolic clutter.

And even if you do have the means to surround yourself with palatial splendor, you must be continually on guard
to see that the result is a true monument to your style. If it
becomes simply a celebration of your affluence—or, worse, an
advertisement for your "success"—it will be a joke. And the
joke will be on your claim to style. William Randolph
Hearst, in creating San Simeon, understood this. Hugh
Hefner, in creating the Playboy Mansions, did not.

Having settled on your particular style in nest-building,
it is of course important that you stay with it. Frequent
scenery changes are confusing and distracting. Obviously this
does not mean that you must keep every element of your
domicile in place for eternity, but it does mean that you must
never change the special quality of your surroundings.

Along the same lines, it is a good idea to maintain your
place at all times in the same state of tidiness or disarray,
cleanliness or uncleanliness. Hastily dusting or tidying up for
visitors is a form of lying. Besides, it doesn't fool anybody.
Being a little bit messy is like being a little bit pregnant, so

it's silly to try to hide it. In fact, it is better to go all the way and be comprehensively messy (or maniacally fastidious) and thereby eliminate the possibility of inconsistency.

Finally, a word about the neighbors. Robert Frost said it all when he wrote, "Good fences make good neighbors." You must have some barriers—either physical or metaphorical, or both—between you and the neighbors. It is always very tempting to make friends with the nice people next door simply because they *are* nice and they *are* next door, but that is precisely why you should *not* allow them to get too close to you. They are close enough already, and if you invite them in you run the risk of launching a perpetual cycle of reciprocal invitations that can end only in boredom or embarrassment or, in some cases, outright hostility. So keep what little distance you have from them—with courtesy and cordiality, of course—and you won't have to worry later about them crowding your style.

TEST YOUR
STYLE QUOTIENT

1. If you are a stylist, you will dislike the place where you live because:

   (a) It is uncomfortable.
   (b) It is too expensive.
   (c) It misrepresents you.
   (d) Your in-laws also live there.

2. If you are a stylist, you will live in a small town because:

   (a) You were born there.
   (b) You like the slower pace of a small town.

(c) You like gossip.
(d) You like the greater notoriety you can attract.

3. If you are a stylist, you will approve of floral wallpaper because:

   (a) It's already on the wall.
   (b) You bought it on sale.
   (c) You are indifferent to matters of taste.
   (d) It is in somebody else's house so you don't have to look at it.

4. If you are a stylist, you will keep the curtains drawn because:

   (a) You like privacy.
   (b) You dislike the outside world.
   (c) You prefer artificial light.
   (d) You want to excite the neighbors' curiosity.

5. If you are a stylist, you will put a picture of your house on your Christmas cards because:

   (a) Your house is quite beautiful.
   (b) Your house is indescribably shabby.
   (c) You want to sell it.
   (d) You painted the picture yourself.

(Answers on page 178)

CREATING A FAMILY

with Style

I

F PROCREATING WITH STYLE is a difficult enough task, creating a stylish family out of the results is a positively Herculean (if not Sisyphean) labor. Indeed, it is almost a law of nature that stylists do not produce stylish offspring. And even when they do, as in the case of Evelyn Waugh and his wonderfully dyspeptic son Auberon, the offspring is condemned to being seen not as the possessor of his own style but merely as the custodian of someone else's.

That is if he is lucky. More often he will be seen as a failed imitator (or an outright repudiator) of the style of the parent. This is inescapable, because he has to live in a world of expectations that have been created by the parents' style. Whether he chooses to try to fulfill those expectations or to reject them, the fact that he carries the name and (presumably) some of the physical features of a stylish parent ensures that comparisons, most of them invidious, will permanently stalk his existence. This is a terrible burden for anyone to bear.

Nor is the burden exclusively on the progeny. While you may cast a long shadow over the style of your children, their style—or lack of it—will equally reflect on you. Only the most conspicuous stylist, or one with the most inconspicuous offspring, will not at some time be found guilty by association. In fact, the very existence of offspring can be hazardous to your image, because you never know when some monstrous caricature will climb out of the family gene pool. Look at Jimmy Carter's son Jeff. Not even David Levine, in his most wicked hallucination, would represent Mr. Carter like that.

These are things to think about, and think about seriously, before deciding to reproduce yourself. Children are, after all, nonreturnable. So you will have to live the rest of your life with the consequences of your decision.

Assuming, however, that you are determined to help populate the world yourself, how can you do it with style? The first thing you should do, appropriately enough, is the first thing you will be *asked* to do: Give the child a name. This is more important than you might imagine. In fact, it is one of the most important decisions you will ever make concerning your child, and thus it merits consideration at some length.

What's in a name? Everything. On the one hand it symbolizes your uniqueness, and on the other it identifies you as a member of various groups—your race, your sex, your nationality, your family (and, often, your generation and social class). It is the one all-purpose handle that the world has on you. It is made up of the only words in the language which, when uttered, conjure up an image of you and nobody else.

Thus it is one of life's little ironies that the job of picking a name for you, initially at least, is one that falls to somebody else. You have no say in the matter whatsoever, because the world is not willing to wait to find out what to call you. As a prospective parent, then, you should give careful consideration to the matter of deciding what the world will call your offspring. Because your decision will not only affect the way the world views your child, it will also have a sizable influence on the way the world sees *you.*

There is no such thing as a stylish name per se. Just as

Raymond Chandler declared that "a good title is the title of a successful book," so a stylish name is the name of a stylist. At the same time there are *unstylish* names which you should avoid lest you create a handicap for your child that may be impossible to overcome.

Firstly, as always, you should avoid fashionable names. It is the surest way of branding your child as part of a herd. This point was splendidly illustrated in a recent *New Yorker* cartoon by Jack Ziegler depicting an elementary school class portrait. The caption read:

> *Last Row:* Scott, Jennifer, Jennifer, Scott, Jennifer, Jennifer, Scott, Scott. *Middle Row:* Jennifer, Jennifer, Scott, Scott, Jennifer, Jennifer, Scott, Jennifer, Scott. *Front Row:* Jennifer, Scott, Scott, Jennifer, Mrs. Wanda Projhieki, Scott, Scott, Scott, Scott.

Secondly, avoid giving your child any name that gratuitously (and perhaps erroneously) identifies him as a member of a group. For example, if you give your children names like Xavier or Bernadette, it will be assumed that you are advertising their—and your—Catholicism. Likewise, names like Sean or Deirdre will be seen as a means of emphasizing their —and your—Irishness. (Or, horror of horrors, they will be seen as an attempt to appropriate the Irishness of others.) And unless you want your children identified as having come from the lower class, you will avoid The Curse of the Y. According to this curse, anyone whose name has been fancied up—usually by the addition or deletion of a *y*, as in Cyndy, Cindi, Lynda, Jayne, Gayle—is certain to be recognized as coming from well down the social ladder. The same is true of anyone unfortunate enough to bear a name that recalls a famous movie star or sports hero. You will never find an Elvis dining at the Harvard Club.

Thirdly, avoid burdening your child with a name that

he will have to live up to—or live down. In the former category are most abstract nouns (Faith, Prudence, Chastity) and most mythical figures (Hercules, Dionysus); in the latter category are the names of places and things. When one hears that Mick Jagger's child will have to bear the nominal stigmata of Jade Jagger, or that Sylvester Stallone's child will be forced to labor under the appellation of Sage Moonblood Stallone, one realizes that cruelty to children is far from being stamped out.

It is also a bad idea to name a child after yourself. To do so is to send a signal to the world, and to the child, that he has been designated as your surrogate, an outrider for your style. Apart from denying him a crucial element of his individuality, this indicates that you need help in making a name for yourself.

By the same token, it is a mistake to go to the other extreme and come up with an obscure or invented name (or a mangled version of a familiar name). If you go too far in trying to bestow uniqueness on your offspring, people will rightly suspect that you are hoping to establish his individuality by decree rather than by style. And of course it is a sign of terminal witlessness, if not perversity, to play jokes with a child's name—Pearl Button, Ima Hogg, that sort of thing. The laughs will be at your expense as well as the child's.

It is advisable, too, to stay away from names that readily lend themselves to unattractive diminutive forms. Diminutives are diminishing, as the artist Robert Rauschenberg recognized many years ago when he changed his name from Milton Rauschenberg just to avoid the awful possibility that he might be called Miltie. And any name that is difficult to pronounce, or that collides rhythmically with the surname, should be dismissed from consideration. For a name to be right it must *sound* right.

It must also be used right. Which means it must be used, period. It is ridiculous to go to the trouble to come up with the right name for a child if you are then going to abbreviate it or substitute a nickname. Abbreviations and nicknames, like diminutives, should always be discouraged because they are essentially deeds of ownership: They are used by people to show that they have a claim on your friendship or affections.

And if you are going to give your offspring more than one name—not a particularly good idea unless you are looking for a cheap way to pay off family debts—be sure to put first the name he will be known by. If you give a child two names and then call him by the second one, he is likely to end up confused as to who he really is. Later, this confusion, as manifested by the awkward placing of an initial in front of the *real* name, will make him easy prey for those who may wish to exploit him for their own sinister ends. It is no coincidence that Richard Nixon, that most predatory of political animals, chose as his confederates men with such names as C. Arnholt Smith, W. Clement Stone, J. Edgar Hoover, L. Patrick Gray, J. Fred Buzhardt, G. Gordon Liddy, and E. Howard Hunt.

E. Nough Said.

A digression is in order here. What if *your* parents, oblivious to the above considerations, sent you out into the world with a name that you feel inhibits or contradicts your style? Simple. Change it. As Judge Learned Hand observed when he granted Samuel Goldfish permission to change his name to Samuel Goldwyn, "A self-made man may prefer a self-made name." And since a stylist is by definition self-made, it is not at all uncommon for people with style to want to take a name which fits that style.

After all, if your style is to ride into town in a cloud of dust, even the horse will have trouble taking you seriously if your name is Leonard Slye or Marion Morrison. Which is why Mr. Slye and Mr. Morrison changed their names to Roy Rogers and John Wayne. And if you want to strike terror in the hearts of your foes, causing them to tremble at the sound of your name, it will be difficult if your name is Dzhugashvili or Schiklgruber. Which is why Mr. Dzhugashvili and Mr. Schiklgruber took the names Stalin and Hitler. If you aspire to become one of the foremost actors in the English-speaking world, you might well consider it a handicap to have a provincial Welsh name. Richard Jenkins did, so he changed his name to Richard Burton. And if you want to be known as a hard-hitting heavyweight, you may have a credibility problem if your name is Arnold Raymond Cream. That's why the witty Mr. Cream became Jersey Joe Walcott.

It doesn't matter whether you change your name drastically or only alter it slightly, so long as the result serves your purpose. The comedian Jacob Cohen opted for the complete overhaul—"I figured," he says, "if you're going to change your name you might as well *change* it"—and turned himself into Rodney Dangerfield. William Claude Dukenfield, on the other hand, only had to do the slightest tinkering to become W. C. Fields. All that matters when it comes to changing your name is that you do it for the sake of your style. Never change it for the sake of a group or a cause. Nor, for that matter, should you *keep* a name just to make a political point. Ladies who insist on keeping their maiden names after marriage, solely to prove how liberated they are, in fact are only proving that they are confused about who they are. Why else would they prefer the name of a man they didn't choose to the name of a man they did choose?

So much for the question of names. Assuming that your children have been appropriately named, your next important job is to keep them under the sway of an enlightened tyranny. If you are going to raise a family with style, there can be no doubts as to who is in charge.

As an enlightened tyrant, your primary responsibility is, of course, to pass on your enlightenment to your offspring. While this involves a certain measure of tedium—for instance having to explain, sometimes repeatedly, why it is that certain activities are universally considered unattractive—it also involves (because you will be teaching mostly by example) the welcome opportunity to practice your style before a captive audience.

In fact, for the stylist one of the few blessings of having children is that they tend to keep you honest. They are always the first to notice—and call attention to—discrepancies between your public and private behavior. Thus they can be quite effective guardians of your style.

Now comes the question of their education. Here your concern should be not so much with the "quality" of the education as with the *kind* of education. It should be designed to expand as far as possible the range of options available to your offspring when they move on. A "good education" is not one that makes it unthinkable that a child should want to be a truck driver; it is one that makes it possible for him to think of something else.

Thus the ideal school is the one with the broadest curriculum, the one that offers your child the best chance to discover who he is and what he might become. And at the heart of the curriculum must be the teaching of language, for at the heart of all style is the use of language. Consequently, a school that excels in teaching children how to use words accurately and interestingly—preferably in several languages—is the one most likely to produce someone who can make himself intelligible to the greatest number of people, and who therefore will have the greatest scope for the exercise of his style.

Not that school is the only medium of education. Television is also an important source of information. Unfortunately, however, the information it imparts, with rare exceptions, has been pre-minced in the Silverman Blender in order to reduce it to such stupefying mediocrity that it can be digested by the feeblest of minds. So the television is best left turned off in the presence of a child, unless you want to run the risk of his suffering brain damage from exposure to toxic waste. Even the cleverest child, after being drenched in Niagaras of canned laughter and benumbed by soap-operatic soundtracks, will come to confuse gag-swapping with humor, earnestness with seriousness.

The baleful ubiquity of television notwithstanding, the most critical nonformal education your child will receive will still come from you. And that education will derive not only from the precepts you lay down but also, and more forcefully, from the example you set. Children may not always hear what you say, but they always watch what you do. It is crucial, therefore, that your actions do not belie your words.

Like the education provided by school, the education provided by you should have one principal purpose: the broadening of options. The more choices a child has in any given situation, the more likely it is that he will make the right one. That is why political or religious indoctrination is a bad idea. If it works, it closes down options rather than increases them. (And if it doesn't work, it still has the same effect, because rebellion against a doctrine is just as narrowly focused as pious adherence to it.) Conversely, this is why instruction in the social graces is a good idea. It gives a child the flexibility of behavior that will be essential when the time comes to put his style to work.

Indeed, the teaching of manners is the single most important contribution that you can make to the style of your offspring. They may not choose to incorporate into their style everything you teach them, but unless you teach them they will not even have a choice in the matter. And since good manners are simply a formalized way of signaling respect for others, the inability to send such a signal will severely limit the type and number of social contacts open to them.

Don't forget that of all the possible excuses for your children's behavior, regardless of the circumstances, the only one that reflects as dismally on you as it does on them is that they didn't know any better.

Whatever they do, as long as they *know* what they're doing, it's not your fault.

TEST YOUR STYLE QUOTIENT

1. If you are a stylist, you will have lots of children because:

   (a) You are Catholic.
   (b) You are careless.
   (c) You want to be supported in your old age.
   (d) You want your style to be supported by agents in the field.

2. If you are a stylist, you will have only one child because:

   (a) You are tired.
   (b) You don't want to divide your attention further.
   (c) You can't afford more than one.
   (d) You learn from your mistakes.

3. If you are a stylist, you will spoil your children because:

   (a) You like them.
   (b) You want them to like you.

(c) You are afraid of them.

(d) You want them to spoil you in return later.

4. If you are a stylist, you will neglect your children because:

   (a) You don't like them.

   (b) You have better things to spend your time on.

   (c) You don't want to interfere with them.

   (d) You want to antagonize your mother-in-law.

5. If you are a stylist, you will buy pets for your children because:

   (a) It will give them a sense of responsibility.

   (b) It will save you having to play with them.

   (c) You want the pets for yourself.

   (d) You want an alternative food supply in case of an economic depression.

(Answers on page 179)

PERFORMING YOUR JOB

with Style

YEATS ONCE WROTE THAT man is forced to choose between perfecting his life or perfecting his work. Yeats was wrong. It is only a matter of which comes first—your life or your work. If you are a stylist, the choice is as easy as it is obvious: Your life comes first. Then you inject it into your work. You bring what you *are* to what you do.

Whatever your job, it should bear the imprint of your personality, not vice versa. Even in a job such as acting, which would seem to demand the submersion of one's individuality in the requirements of different roles, the actor with style will always take over the character he portrays and reshape it in his own image. To take two widely disparate examples, it is impossible to imagine John Wayne or Woody Allen playing anyone but John Wayne and Woody Allen. Similarly, the characters played by Bette Davis and Tallulah Bankhead were invariably overwhelmed by the unique personalities of the actresses themselves. Katharine Hepburn once said, "Show me an actress who isn't a personality and I'll show you a woman who isn't a star." That may be overstating it a bit in these days of instant (and evanescent) stardom, but it is certainly true to say that an actor or actress who isn't a personality can't be a stylist.

It is also true to say that there is no job, in show business or any other business, which will reject the graft of style if you are willing to subordinate it to your personality. At first glance, for instance, what could offer less scope for the superimposition of one's personality than playing the piano or reading the news? Yet when you consider the style that a Liberace or a Victor Borge brings to piano-playing, and the style that a Walter Cronkite or a David Brinkley brings to news-reading, you realize that even the most circumscribed function can be transformed when it is made a part of somebody's special personality.

Johnny Carson is another case in point. On the surface, it would appear that nothing could be better calculated to induce mass catatonia than a late-night television program in which the same person asks the same people the same questions night after night, year after year. Yet Carson has so thoroughly stamped the show with his own unmistakable (and carefully calculated) style that its effect is hypnotic rather than soporific. As a result, after eighteen years on the job, Carson is today more popular than ever.

However big or complex a job may be, it is never too big or too complex to be subdued by the force of personality. Running a large hotel, for example, is a dauntingly involved undertaking; for that very reason, most modern hotels have been streamlined to the point that they are depressingly alike—impersonal, antiseptic, bland. In such a wilderness a hotel like the Beverly Wilshire in Beverly Hills shines out like a beacon, attracting Muzak-crazed travelers who yearn for a place with warmth and elegance and, above all, personality. And personality is what they get: the personality of the hotel's owner, Hernando Courtright. His signature, literally as well as metaphorically, can be seen wherever you look. Everything, from the design of the soap-wrappers to the attitude of the staff, is a direct reflection, as it should be, of

Hernando Courtright's taste and standards. In short, the place has style because Mr. Courtright has style.

Still, running a hotel with style is not a challenge of quite the same magnitude as that of running a country with style. Yet Winston Churchill was able to do it, and in wartime at that. In these days of highly visible, elaborately staged "crisis management," when political leaders anxiously watch the public opinion polls to see which way the wind is blowing, and then consult their media advisers to find out how far they can bend with the wind without exposing their haunches, it is salutary to remember that when the British were fighting for their very survival Churchill directed that fight from his bed, brandy and cigars to hand. It wasn't that he was ill or fatigued; he just liked working in bed. He liked his little naps, too. And he was frequently known to adjourn emergency cabinet meetings in order to linger over a particularly satisfying lunch. In other words, he met the demands of office on *his* terms, in the context of *his* requirements.

Anyone who leads his nation to victory in history's most calamitous war, all the while refusing to allow that war to interfere with his style, must be regarded as one of the supreme models of a stylist at work.

One should keep in mind, however, that these examples are all of people who brought their style to their jobs. When you look at people who took on a style as part of the job, you see a different picture altogether. Perhaps the outstanding example of this unhappy predicament is provided by Queen Elizabeth. Although she is by birth the sovereign monarch of a once mighty empire, and one of the richest women in the world as well, her *job* is to be unassuming, middle-class, housewifely, and to make quite certain that she doesn't meddle in anything important. Admittedly, she discharges these duties with grace and dignity, but at the same time she is precluded from having any style of her own whatsoever. As a consequence, she inspires in us little more than that belated curiosity we have about all creatures whom we are helping toward extinction.

Judy Garland was another who acquired her style along with her job. In her case the style, and the job, were provided by Louis B. Mayer, who persuaded her—no, told her—that to be successful she would have to remake herself to conform to the image he had in mind for her. Which she did, with the melancholy result that by the time she died at the age of forty-seven she had long since burnt herself out, without ever having a chance to discover who she really was.

Where the Queen's job-style was imposed by the people, with a nervous eye on the past, and Judy Garland's was imposed by a person, with a beady eye on the profits, Hugh Hefner's has been imposed by himself, with a bloodshot eye on his fantasies about what the life of a playboy must be like. Nonetheless, it is a style that came with the job—even though the job, editing and publishing *Playboy,* is one that Hefner created—and not a style that he *brought* to the job. Thus, as Hefner became more prosperous he became more preposterous, letting his style be dictated by his quaint notions of what it is to be a playboy. He got himself a big wardrobe (which of course featured lots of gaudy silk shirts), a big airplane (which of course he had painted black), a big house (which of course he called a "mansion"), a big bed (which of course was circular), some big mirrors (which of course were placed on the ceiling), a big stereo set (which of course filled the premises with such seductive classics as "Tie A Yellow Ribbon"), and a big staff (which of course was expected to serve the hamburgers and Pepsis at all hours of the night). Then he installed a herd of bovine post-adolescents with names like Barbi, Nanci, Bobbi, Sandi, who of course were willing to submit to his concupiscent heavings and gropings in hopes of getting a chance to appear in the magazine or—gosh!—the movies. (Actually, they did get the chance to appear on television, albeit before a limited audience, because Hefner also had installed a closed-circuit television camera and screen above his bed so that he could catch himself in the act—and, presumably, thereby convince himself that he really was a playboy.) Ah, the style of a sophisticate!

Laughable as all this may be, however, it does point up the hazards of letting your job affect your style rather than having your style affect your job. If you are going to perform a job with style, you must have the style before you have the job.

Of course, the extent to which you can apply your style to the performance of a job depends in large part on the type of job you choose. Clearly, those jobs which put you in front of the largest number of people—acting, singing, teaching, preaching; in a word, performing—offer the greatest scope for exhibiting your stylistic talents. As a general rule, therefore, those jobs which allow you to "do" something are to be preferred over those which require you to "make" something. The best job for a stylist is one where your personality is your product.

Even so, it is possible to make things for a living without forsaking your style. Ernest Hemingway made novels, for example, but he also made himself the prototypical Hemingway hero: a rugged man of action, a courageous and intrepid hunter who shot every sort of game, including, ultimately, himself. Norman Mailer took the process one stage further by not only being Maileresque, but also by making himself the explicit hero of some of his books. Hunter Thompson and Tom Wolfe have done much the same thing, though Wolfe has added a new twist: He has developed a prose style (and a style of dress to go with it) that implies a certain ironic detachment from the world he writes about. Similarly, those columnists with the greatest style—whether their columns deal in gossip, fact, or opinion—are the ones who have put themselves at the center of their work.

By contrast, those who are content with more or less objective reportage forfeit the opportunity to apply their style to their job, which means that when they lose their job they lose virtually everything by which the world identifies them, as evidenced by the cruel little story that United Press International put out when columnist Pete Hamill was abruptly dismissed by his newspaper. "Pete Hamill has been fired from his job as columnist for the New York *Daily News*," the story said. "Hamill's claims to fame have been several novels and a friendship with Jacqueline Kennedy Onassis."

But writers are by no means the only ones who have found ways to imprint their personalities on their products. Artists, too, have sometimes managed to make their lives their principal works of art, so that everything they produce becomes a kind of self-portrait, an updated bulletin on a life in progress. Andy Warhol and David Hockney are excellent examples of such artists. So is Salvador Dali, whose surrealist works are perfect emblems of his surreal life and appearance. Emphasizing the noncoincidental nature of this connection, Dali has said: "The difference between a madman and me is that I am not mad." Indeed he is not. As the critic Robert Hughes has pointed out, "Everything is calculated, literally down to the last hair: even his mustache is lifted from Velasquez's portraits of Philip IV."

Artists such as the German Joseph Beuys and the American Chris Burden have gone even further in erasing the distinction between their life and art. Both have put frames, as it were, around events in their lives, so that the moment of *being* an artist becomes the art itself. In other words, they have tried to show that you can produce art without necessarily producing an artifact. This may strike many as a strange notion, but the great modern master himself, Picasso, would have understood. In fact, it could be said that, as with so many other aspects of contemporary art, Picasso was the first to appreciate the fact that the images an artist creates might be linked to—indeed be considered inseparable from —the image of the artist himself. For it was Picasso, a great stylist as well as a great artist, who said of himself, "I am only an entertainer who has understood his time."

These examples notwithstanding, it is still better to look for a job that encourages the *direct* expression of your personality instead of requiring the production of things which have to be somehow crafted in your image. Your craftsmanship is better spent on yourself than on things. And, ideally, the job should be one that lends itself to your particular style. Boxing, for example, is a job that not only demands pugilistic skill but also requires a degree of bravura and psychological gamesmanship. Thus it was made for someone like Muhammad Ali. Likewise, what could be a more appropriate destiny for a celluloid fairy princess like Grace Kelly than to end up as a real-life fairy princess in a fairy kingdom?

Surely, though, the perfect example of someone who found a job to match his style is Pope John Paul II. Like Pope John XXIII, the only other pope in living memory to have style, he brought to the papacy the humility and charm to carry out his pastoral duties as the gentle shepherd of a giant flock, and at the same time the sense of uncompromising strength and authority to be His Holiness the Supreme Pontiff, the doctrinally infallible successor of St. Peter. When God created the job, He must have had Karol Wojtyla in mind.

Unfortunately, the rest of us must settle for somewhat less perfect jobs. But that doesn't mean you should settle for any job at all, on the theory that you can always change it with your style. It is easier to be unemployed with style than it is to be a stylist in the wrong job. What jobs are wrong for a stylist? To start with, any job that does not require you to speak while performing it clearly offers little opportunity for you to display your style. (The one exception is modeling, where facial and body language become substitutes for speech.) This means that you should avoid most forms of manual labor as well as those office jobs where someone *else* does all the talking. (Remember G. K. Chesterton's derisive comment: "Twenty million young women rose to their feet with the cry, 'We will not be dictated to,' and promptly became stenographers.") Secondly, avoid working for any company so large and impersonal that you are unknown to your employer. Anonymity and style are incompatible. Lastly, avoid any occupation that requires membership of a union. If you can command attention only as part of a group, or find job safety only in numbers, then you should abandon any notion of being a stylist in your work.

As with choosing a type of clothing or housing, so with choosing a line of work: Once you have made your choice, stay with it. While it is sometimes a good idea to change jobs (so long as you don't do it too often), it is always a bad idea to change occupations. Consider the example of Stanley Marcus, a man who indisputably had style when he was head of Neiman-Marcus. After he stepped down, he wrote a book about himself and his store, which was fine. Then he wrote another book, which would have been fine too, except that he wrote it because he thought that if he wrote *two* books he would then be "considered an author." He was wrong.

Nor should you change the style with which you perform your job. David Frost made this mistake. He rose to fame as a deadpan satirist and an incisive interviewer, but apparently he decided that he would rather consort with the famous than be famous in his own right as a performer with style. Whereupon he changed from being a skeptical interrogator to being an awestruck groupie. The price of his conversion was the loss of his style.

Another trap into which many people fall is the temptation to think of a job as simply a means to an end, a way of putting food on the table. Such an attitude is guaranteed to make your job boring, because it deprives you of the sort of commitment and enthusiasm that alone can redeem the drudgery and disappointment which are built into every kind of work.

It is a mistake, too, to fall for the theological view of work: that it is a form of suffering to be endured for the sake of rewards in the hereafter. Even if you are certain that you will have a future that needs to be provided for, by the time you get there any style you might have had will have been crushed under the weight of the compromises you will have been forced to make in the name of "providing for your future."

Nor should you ever ask for more money on the grounds that someone else doing comparable work is being better compensated than you are. For one thing, a stylist never compares himself to others. For another, to demand equal pay is to ask to be treated the same as others—and no stylist wants to be treated the same as other people.

And it should go without saying that no stylist either glorifies or makes excuses for his job. If you are a garbage collector, don't call yourself a sanitation engineer. If you are a secretary, don't announce that you are the executive secretary to the senior vice-president of the largest whatnot in town. Just say that you are a secretary, or describe what you do in the simplest terms (preferably with humor). Likewise, if you consider your job unworthy of your talents, or perhaps a step down from your last position, don't try to explain how you happened to take the job. No job is so lowly that it cannot be done with style, and if you appear to be ashamed of your job it will reflect unfavorably on your style, not on your job.

Finally, you should never fret about your talents being inadequate for the job. Sarah Bernhardt was a dreadful actress: Her fame testified to the greatness of her style rather than to the quality of her acting. Similarly, Eva Peron had no more political sophistication than one would expect of an ex-chorus girl, but so great was her style that elementary school primers in Argentina began with the words, "I love Evita." And certainly no one would argue that Muhammad Ali's fame as a boxer rests primarily on his punching ability, or that the legend of El Cordobes was built on his skill in the art of bullfighting.

So remember that whatever work you choose to do, it will be your talents as a stylist rather than your skills as a worker that will determine whether you succeed in performing the job with style.

TEST YOUR STYLE QUOTIENT

1. If you are a stylist, you will become an accountant because:

   (a) You want to find out if your business associates are cheating you.
   (b) You consider counting money the next best thing to having it.
   (c) You consider figures easier to manage than people.
   (d) In accountancy your mistakes are so noticeable.

2. If you are a stylist, you will work at home because:

   (a) You dislike having to take public transport.
   (b) You prefer your own environment to anyone else's.
   (c) You want to be able to answer the telephone when your friends call.
   (d) Nobody can see how little you do.

3. If you are a stylist, you will work at night because:

   (a) You will never be expected to entertain.
   (b) You will work with more interesting people.
   (c) You have insomnia.
   (d) You are a cat burglar.

4. If you are a stylist, you will be slow to finish your work because:

   (a) You enjoy it and don't want it to end.
   (b) You want to be paid for overtime.
   (c) You are conscientious.
   (d) You have nowhere to go when the work is completed.

5. If you are a stylist, you will be out of work because:

   (a) You want the time free for spending with other people.
   (b) You are too good for the jobs available.
   (c) You have found public welfare to be more lucrative.
   (d) You are lazy.

(Answers on page 179)

ENTERTAINING YOUR FRIENDS

with Style

EVEN AMONG STYLISTS THERE
are two different views as to the real purpose of entertaining.
According to one view, entertaining is simply a convenient
means of showing off. It is a way of economizing on time and
effort by assembling around you a number of people for
whom you might otherwise have to budget a considerable
amount of energy in order to reach.

With this approach, there is no attempt made to limit
your entertaining to your circle of friends. On the contrary,
the whole point is to expose yourself to people who are *not*
already your friends. This means following the prescription
of George Eliot in *Daniel Deronda*: "Hostesses who entertain must make up their parties as ministers make up their
cabinets, on grounds other than personal liking." In fact, you
might go even further and heed the Biblical advice of He-
brews 13:2—"Be not forgetful to entertain strangers: for
thereby some have entertained angels unawares."

The other view of entertaining holds that it is a gift—of
relaxation and amusement—that you bestow on those whose
company you enjoy, without regard to their qualifications as
an audience.

We incline toward this latter view, at the same time
recognizing that there is an irreducible modicum of self-

celebration and showmanship involved whenever you invite people to congregate in your presence and partake of your hospitality. There is always an element of courtiers being summoned to the court, regardless of the occasion or the reason for the party. Nonetheless, the purpose of entertaining should be to reward friendship by making people feel good about being around you.

This more limited approach to entertaining has two advantages. In the first place, by restricting your guest list to friends, you won't put yourself in the position of having to suffer fools gladly, or at all. In the second place, by restricting the *kind* of entertaining you do, you ensure that it will serve your style rather than *become* your style.

Anyone who entertains on a large scale, or very often, runs the risk of becoming identified in the eyes of the world as a host or hostess first and a stylist second. Such a fate befell Misia Sert, a lady whose charm once held in thrall many of the great figures of the Belle Epoque in Paris, including Stravinsky, Ravel, Diaghilev, Proust, Mallarmé, Colette, Toulouse-Lautrec, and Renoir. For years she held open house every day of the week, but eventually the time came when her glittering companions stopped showing up. And as they disappeared from her life so did her style, for her style, like her glory, was reflected. Even her husbands (three of them in succession) deserted her for other women. She died in 1950 a broken, lonely figure.

But it doesn't take a sad decline to illustrate the hollowness of a style built around entertaining. Perle Mesta and Elsa Maxwell are good examples of what happens to people for whom entertaining is a style in itself: As far as the world was concerned, when these ladies weren't giving parties they ceased to exist. No wonder, then, that when Cecil Beaton's *Book of Beauty* was published in 1930 it so enraged Lady Cunard that she threw her complimentary copy into the fire.

"He calls me a *hostess*," she fumed. "That shows he's a low fellow!"

To entertain with style requires that the host or hostess be at once passive and attentive. You must never try to dominate the proceedings, or it will appear that the only kind of audience whose attention you can command is one that you assemble yourself. At the same time you must be attentive and alert to the needs of your guests. That is to say, you should act like a host and not like just another guest. When Truman Capote threw a lavish fancy dress ball for *Washington Post* publisher Katharine Graham in 1966, at a cost of $75,000, it was noted that Capote himself dressed and carried on as if he were one of the guests. Indeed, he said that his reason for mounting the affair was so that he could go to a party where he could have a really good time. This led, understandably, to the twin suspicions that what Capote really wanted was an occasion where he could upstage the other guests, and that if he had to spend that much money in order to get it (or simply to have a good time) then something was seriously missing in his style.

Another rule for entertaining with style is never to give a party so large that everyone there cannot be made fully aware of your presence. It's pointless to go to the trouble to bring people together and then, because of the pressure of numbers, be forced to withhold yourself from some of them. If you cannot give them the sort of attention that makes it uniquely *your* party, you might as well invite them to go to somebody else's party. Besides, in an overly large group of people you will be cheated out of one of the principal pleasures of entertaining. As Aeschylus said many centuries ago, there is nothing "pleasanter than the tie of host and guest," but you can only create and maintain that tie with a limited number of people at once. If you try to do it with too many people, you will end up losing it with all of them.

There are problems, too, with giving parties that are too small. For one thing, the more intimate affairs require a higher level of social poise and concentration than do parties of, say, twelve or more. Your poise will be more severely tested because you come under closer scrutiny in smaller gatherings. And the demands on your concentration will be greater because the fewer the people, the larger the claim each has on your attention. Still, none of this should unduly concern the true stylist. Tallulah Bankhead used to hold little cocktail parties in her bathroom, sometimes without bothering to dress first, and *her* style survived the scrutiny.

When entertaining, a stylist will always take care to avoid inadvertently embarrassing or intimidating his guests. Take the matter of clothes, for instance. You should be slightly more simply dressed than your guests. You dress up for *other people's* parties; you dress down for your own. Remember that your first duty as a host is to make people feel comfortable, and no one feels comfortable who feels under-dressed.

Nor do people feel comfortable when they feel "paired off" with other people, or other couples, according to some prearranged design. Therefore, guest lists should never be compiled with a view to getting equal representation according to gender, nor should your guests, if it's a dinner party, be forced to sit according to some arbitrary boy-girl-boy-girl format. They should be allowed to sit where and with whom they please. Indeed, the furniture itself should be arranged in such a way as to encourage casualness and spontaneity. A great French lady, fabled for her style as a hostess, once claimed that the secret of her success lay in the seemingly random organization of her furniture. "An entertaining conversation," she explained, "can never begin in a salon where the furniture is symmetrically arranged."

In short, anything that smacks of predetermined order

tends to create an atmosphere of uneasiness, of unspoken expectations, and that is not the sort of atmosphere you want to create.

As good conversation is the key ingredient in any good party, it is essential for those who would entertain with style to cultivate a rare skill: the ability to listen properly. This ability, as we pointed out in our chapter on speaking with style, is important to a stylist in any situation, but when you are a host it is absolutely crucial. Almost without exception, all of the great hosts and hostesses of history have also been great listeners. Madame Récamier, who presided over a legendary salon in the early nineteenth century, is said to have hardly ever uttered a word. This doesn't mean that you need to take a vow of silence in order to be a great host, but you do need an infinite capacity for listening to other people's stories without retaliating with stories of your own.

As far as conversational topics are concerned, the only ones which should be avoided are those which are likely to exclude people (shop talk, for instance) or antagonize them (such as certain religious or political opinions) or otherwise make them ill at ease (which would include most revelations about one's personal relationships). Ideally, a conversation should be steered in the direction of a subject or subjects on which everyone has a view, for these are the subjects most apt to produce the sort of spirited exchanges that every host recognizes as the hallmark of a successful party.

On the question of whether to provide music, it obviously depends on the type of occasion. In general, though, the sound of a good party is not the sound of music but the sound of people. If you nonetheless feel the need for some background music, at least make sure that it *stays* in the background. It should be aural wallpaper, muted and neutral. If it is too loud or too pulsing, so that people have to talk over it, it will obliterate any style that you may have given to the occasion. Don't forget that when you raise the level of noise you automatically lower the level of conversation. Nobody is interesting when he's shouting.

If you intend to serve food, see to it that it is served *on time*—which means fairly early on. Not only is it inconsiderate to make your guests go hungry after having invited them for a meal, but it is also risky, for it encourages them to drink too much, which in turn tends to make them edgy and shrill. This can happen in even the best company. Fidel Castro will attest to that. In October 1979, on the last evening of his visit to New York to address the United Nations, Castro gave a dinner party at the Cuban mission for the mandarins of the American news media. His intention clearly was to polish up his image with the most powerful network executives and newspaper editors in the country. However, he got so carried away by the sound of his own voice (not for the first time) that he neglected to ask for dinner to be served until eleven o'clock, by which time the sound of his voice was all but drowned out by the strident voices of his guests, driven to the edge of panic by the looming specter of starvation. Such was the din that one guest later described the evening as sounding "like a Fellini movie." Thus did an attempted public relations coup become a debacle and, afterward, a standing joke.

But even if a late dinner didn't carry such risks it would still be a bad idea, because it shortens the time available for the most enjoyable part of the evening. No cocktail chatter can ever be as relaxed and convivial as the conversation that takes place during and after dinner. So don't delay in getting people to the table.

Finally, at the end of the evening, don't delay their departure. Getting people to leave is much harder than getting them to come in the first place. So unless you want your guests to become an army of occupation, you must resist the temptation to prolong the occasion beyond its natural term. When people say that it's time for them to go, don't argue. Tell them how marvelous it has been to see them, and make a move toward ushering them out. With those who repeatedly miss their cue, a little nudging may be called for.

This is perfectly proper, for the moment entertaining becomes tiresome or obligatory it becomes something other than entertaining. And it will be handled with something other than style.

TEST YOUR STYLE QUOTIENT

1. If you are a stylist, you will throw a party for 15,000 people because:

    (a) You want to show that you know 15,000 people.
    (b) You want to deal with everybody all at once.
    (c) You don't want to deal with anybody individually.
    (d) You want to see what will happen.

2. If you are a stylist, you will refrain from entertaining because:

    (a) It is too costly.
    (b) It is unnecessary.
    (c) It ruins the house.
    (d) It exposes you to the tedium of reciprocal hospitality.

3. If you are a stylist, you will be overdressed for your own party because:

(a) You are always overdressed.

(b) You want to send a message to those whom you consider underdressed.

(c) You want to dress to match your mood.

(d) You don't have anything else to wear.

4. If you are a stylist, you will dominate the conversation at the dinner table because:

(a) You want to show that you can.

(b) You want to avoid a more boring conversation.

(c) You want to keep your guests from getting to know each other.

(d) You enjoy the sound of your own voice.

5. If you are a stylist, you will serve champagne in plastic cups because:

(a) It saves money.

(b) You care only about how the champagne tastes.

(c) You are in the business of manufacturing plastic cups.

(d) You like to cause comment.

(Answers on page 179)

CONFUSING YOUR ENEMIES

with Style

YOU MIGHT AS WELL FACE it: If you have style, you are going to have enemies. There will be people who will resent you—not for what you do, but for being who you are. Your very existence will be sufficient to arouse hostility. This is inescapable because any personality distinctive enough to attract some people is also going to repel other people. So you had better be prepared for dealing with them.

The first thing to remember, in dealing with aggression or unpleasantness in others, is never to retaliate. Whatever the provocation, a stylist never responds in kind. Your style is designed to work *for* you, not *against* someone else. Moreover, to fight with someone is to insist on something; and a stylist never insists on anything.

But perhaps the most compelling argument against retaliation is that it damages you more than the person at whom it is directed. Notice how in sporting contests it is always the player who throws the *second* punch who gets penalized. The same principle applies to other types of feuds. Nobody remembers what Earl Wilson or Maxine Cheshire or Lee Mortimer or Liz Smith did to provoke Frank Sinatra, but everybody remembers the nastiness of Sinatra's reaction in each case.

The second rule to follow is never to seek compensation

for the actions of your enemies. This means, in particular, that you should never sue for libel. For one thing, by suing you put yourself in a legal contest with someone—and a stylist never competes. Secondly, a libel action requires that you put a price tag on your honor, or credibility, or reputation, or whatever it is that you think has been damaged—and a stylist never sees his worth in monetary terms. To do so is to become like the girl in the old Shavian joke who agrees to go to bed with a man for a million dollars, but angrily refuses when he reduces the offer to one dollar. "What do you think I am?" she asks, outraged. "We've already established what you are," the man replies. "Now we're haggling over the price."

Another reason for avoiding libel actions is that they lend a kind of perverse credibility to that which you consider libelous. Hence the saying, "The greater the truth, the greater the libel." Even if people don't necessarily believe that, they do tend to believe (to quote another familiar saying) that where there's smoke, there's fire. Thus, for example, when *Penthouse* publisher Bob Guccione sued *Hustler* magazine for $80 million after *Hustler* rather crudely suggested that Guccione had homosexual leanings, many people naturally wondered why it was worth so much to Guccione not to be thought to have been infected by the dreaded curse of homosexuality.

Another ironic and unwanted byproduct of libel actions is that they keep the issue alive and guarantee it much wider exposure than it would have had if allowed to drop. Perhaps the most glaring contemporary example of this concerns an interview which Truman Capote gave *Playgirl* magazine back in 1975, in the course of which Capote mentioned that at a party in the White House in 1961, Gore Vidal became so intoxicated and insulting that Robert Kennedy had him thrown out. Now it must be said that as accusations go this one was fairly harmless, but it so enraged Vidal that he sued

Capote for a million dollars. As a result, a little scrap of gossip that would otherwise have been long forgotten is instead, over five years later, still the subject of courtroom wrangling and magazine articles.

In any event, it is impossible to get a satisfactory verdict in a libel case. On the one hand, if the court rules against you, you will have been in effect found guilty of whatever was said about you. (Remember that Oscar Wilde came to his sad end as a direct result of his unsuccessful libel suit against the Marquis of Queensberry.) On the other hand, if the court rules in your favor, it will then in its award place a precise monetary value on your character—a mortifying experience for anyone who *has* any character. This point was gleefully grasped by one Thurlow Weed, a nineteenth-century journalist who was successfully sued for libel by the novelist James Fenimore Cooper. After the verdict and the award of four hundred dollars was announced, Weed exulted: "The value of Mr. Cooper's character has been judicially determined. It is worth exactly four hundred dollars."

In the circumstances, Cooper's reaction might well have echoed the famous sentiments of King Pyrrhus: "Another such victory and I shall be ruined."

As unstylish as it is to seek compensation for having been referred to in an uncomplimentary manner, it is worse to seek revenge. Revenge is merely the process of "getting even"—and no one with style would ever want to be *even* with his enemies. Indeed, the desire to get even is so deranging in itself that simply *wishing* for revenge loosens your grip on yourself. And then it is an easy slide into the sort of pathological vindictiveness that was the undoing of Richard Nixon, for example, and Idi Amin.

That is no exaggeration. One of the most insidious aspects of a taste for revenge is that it's habit-forming. One vengeful act invariably begets another. We have already seen how, following their 1968 television spat, William F. Buckley, Jr. and Gore Vidal embarked on a campaign of getting even with each other. And we have seen how Vidal has now turned his litigious attention to Truman Capote (with manic glee, it would appear, for he has been widely quoted as saying to friends, "I'm looking forward to getting that little toad"). But probably the most appalling recent illustration of how vengefulness can become addictive is provided by Frank Sinatra's continuing vendetta against his critics in the press. So pitifully obsessed is he with his imagined enemies that he even interrupted a 1980 Carnegie Hall concert in order to say nasty things about New York columnist Liz Smith. *That* is how bad it can get.

Retaliation, litigation, revenge: There are no better ways of acknowledging the power of your enemies while at the same time admitting your powerlessness to handle them with style.

So how *do* you deal with them? Basically, your strategy should be not to return their fire but to spike their guns: to make sure that they blow themselves up with their own ammunition. Voltaire once said, "I have never made but one prayer to God, a very short one: 'O Lord, make my enemies ridiculous.' And God granted it." It may come as a surprise, but that is the one prayer that God is always willing to grant, provided that you are prepared to do your part in making your enemies ridiculous.

One way is to employ what might be called the formalist approach. With this, you concentrate exclusively on the *form* of the accusation or insult to which you have been subjected. Voltaire himself was a master of this technique. Once, upon receiving an impudent letter from another gentleman, he ignored the contents of the letter altogether and instead addressed himself in his reply to the circumstances surrounding the disposition of the letter. "Sir," he wrote, "I am seated in the smallest room in the house. I have your letter before me. Soon it will be behind me."

A variation on this technique is exemplified by the recent response of a well-known writer to an extremely abusive letter from another writer of considerably less renown. Rather than deal with the charges and insults contained in the letter, he simply corrected the letter's grammar, spelling, and punctuation, made a few marginal annotations regarding his correspondent's excessive reliance on adjectives, and sent it back with an encouraging comment: "Not bad for a first effort. Not bad at all." Similarly, an insult delivered orally can be returned to sender—unopened, as it were—by simply admiring it *as an insult:* "Good. Very good. I must use that one myself sometime."

A second technique is to meet unpleasant remarks with contrived, even perverse, literalism. Here you focus on the precise, literal meaning of what has been said to or about you, and then exploit the remark's built-in ambiguity—*every* remark is ambiguous on some level—as the basis for a tactical lack of comprehension. The classic model for this sort of contrived confusion is the traditional Yiddish retort, where what has been said is twisted out of shape and returned as a question:

Close the door! It's cold outside.
If I close the door it will be warm outside?

Of course, when represented by a joke, as above, the technique seems a harmless form of entertainment. But when it is used to turn back aggression—"I know your type!" "Often?"; "You're not going to get away with that!" "Who is, then?"—the laugh is on the aggressor.

One of the most delightful examples of exploiting the ambiguity in an antagonistic remark by taking it literally occurred a few years ago when British Prime Minister Harold Wilson was campaigning for reelection. One day in the middle of a speech Mr. Wilson was interrupted by a heckler who jumped up and started shouting "Rubbish!" Smiling tolerantly, Wilson turned to the man and said, "I'll get to your special interest in a moment, sir." (By contrast, when Vice-President Nelson Rockefeller was confronted with an almost identical situation during a campaign speech, he became so enraged at the heckler that he let his finger do the talking. But then Mr. Rockefeller was a man peculiarly lacking in style.)

For those who would prefer a gentler, less demanding technique for dealing with antagonists, there is always The Other Cheek. Two thousand years after Jesus of Nazareth perfected it, this remains one of the most effective ploys ever devised for demoralizing one's enemies. All it takes is a bit of patience and a willingness to agree benignly with everything that is said about you. In fact, if you can manage to keep a straight face, you can take this technique a stage further by earnestly enquiring of your critic what other faults of yours he might have noticed. You can even volunteer a few of your own, just to add to his confusion.

As an adjunct of this technique, it is always a good idea to speak glowingly of those who would malign you. Nothing is so unsettling as to hear that someone you despise is taking every opportunity to express his affection and admiration for you. Moreover, by speaking well of someone who speaks ill of you, you create an uncomfortable dilemma for him—for if he is right in having a low opinion of you, then he must accept that you are wrong in having a high opinion of *him*. Thus he will be forced to revise either his view of you or his view of himself. And in the meantime the implications of the contrast between your kind words behind his back and his unkind words behind *your* back will not be lost on those who know you both.

Finally, whenever you find yourself confronted with an unpleasant remark, remember that you don't have to say anything at all in order to leave your enemy hoisted with his own petard. As George Bernard Shaw said, "Silence is the perfect expression of scorn." Especially if it is accompanied by a sweet smile.

Still, mixed with your silent scorn should be silent acknowledgment of the useful services that your enemies perform. In the first place, they see to it that you are talked about—and that, as Oscar Wilde noted, is much better than *not* being talked about. In the second place, they are willing to tell you things about yourself that nobody else is willing to tell you—and whether accurate or not, such things provide valuable clues to the sort of image that you project. In the third place, the very existence of enemies offers the only indisputable proof that your personality is having the degree of impact (if not necessarily the *type* of impact) that a stylist wants.

So be grateful rather than regretful if you have a few enemies: They come with the territory. Indeed, they are often harder to replace than friends are. As Truman Capote observed, explaining why he thought Gore Vidal would miss him when he's gone: "You can lose a lot of friends but it's hard to lose a good enemy."

Jesus perhaps went a bit far when he said to love your enemies, but certainly you should appreciate them. They are, after all, a part of your style.

TEST YOUR
STYLE QUOTIENT

1. If you are a stylist, you will reply to an insult because:

   (*a*) The insult was unwarranted.
   (*b*) You have something wonderful to say.
   (*c*) You have a line that you want to try out.
   (*d*) You see the promise of a stimulating conversation.

2. If you are a stylist, you will deny an accusation because:

   (a) It was false.
   (b) It was true.
   (c) It was widely repeated.
   (d) It was not widely repeated.

3. If you are a stylist, you will disappear after learning of your mate's infidelity because:

   (a) You want to avoid unpleasantness.
   (b) You want to avoid future surprises.
   (c) You want to create a mystery.
   (d) You have somewhere better to go.

4. If you are a stylist, you will refuse to divulge any financial information to a tax inspector because:

   (a) You don't have any.
   (b) You wish to prolong the confrontation for the fun of it.
   (c) You need time to cook the books.
   (d) You do not wish to go to jail.

5. If you are a stylist, you will run from a policeman because:

   (a) You don't want to be caught.
   (b) You want to make him earn his salary.
   (c) You want to give him some exercise.
   (d) You want to dramatize the situation.

(Answers on page 179)

BEING POOR

with Style

WE TRUST THAT BY NOW WE have made the point that there is no correlation between the amount of style you have and the amount of money you have. Your style does not prosper or suffer according to your cash flow. Nonetheless, the question arises: Is it possible to be poor, *really poor,* with style?

It is. As a matter of fact, it is easier to be a stylist in abject poverty than in less straitened circumstances. For once you start moving up the economic ladder, there is a natural tendency to begin concentrating more and more on the ladder and your position on it, and therefore to begin defining yourself in terms of the people above you and below you. Such a self-image is the antithesis of style.

Since a stylist is in many ways a calculated extremist, it only follows that his style should flourish under extreme conditions—extreme pressure, for example, or extreme danger. The same is true of extreme poverty: It constitutes the sort of milieu in which one's style, or lack of it, is most dramatically in evidence. Of course, we have been so conditioned to think of poverty as an unqualified disaster that few people can even contemplate the idea of an impoverished existence without a sense of dread. To be sure, the pleasures of poverty are few, and the pain of poverty can be considerable, but only if you acknowledge it as such. Pain, like pleasure, is totally subjective, so it is up to each individual to decide for himself whether an experience is painful or not. Nothing is *automatically* painful. The eccentric G. Gordon Liddy used to demonstrate this most graphically at parties by holding his hand over a burning candle until his flesh was seared. When asked what the trick was, he would explain by quoting T. E. Lawrence's line: "The trick is not minding."

So it is with being poor. To be poor with style you must not mind that you are poor.

If this sounds like an impossible precondition, it is only because most of us have been infected by the disease of covetousness, which is pandemic nowadays. We want things not because we need them, but because it pains us to see others have them when we don't. We are uncomprehending when we read in the Talmud that a rich man is "He who is satisfied with what he has," or when Shakespeare writes, in *Othello*, that "poor and content is rich." Surely, we think, "poor and content" is a contradiction. How is it possible to be both poor and content at the same time?

It is only in this century that one could have posed such a question. In earlier times, when one's station in life was more or less foreordained, the poor were largely spared the longing and the disappointment that torment those whose self-esteem is grounded in acquisitiveness. The good life for them was not simply a life full of goods. In modern times, however, the poor have been engulfed by a tidal wave of consumerism, itself whipped by the cruel winds of a bogus egalitarianism, which has meant that they no longer think of themselves in terms of who they are but in terms of what they *have* (and, even more, in terms of what they *don't* have). Sociologists have even validated this peculiar form of misery by referring to the poor as Have-Nots, as distinct from the Haves. No matter that for centuries the world's richest potentates got along quite nicely without the benefit of transistor radios; now the poorest ghetto youth considers himself deprived if he is without one. And this feeling of deprivation derives exclusively from the fact that his friends have them and he doesn't.

Admittedly, in an age when an entire industry is devoted to reminding you of the things you don't have, it is not easy to remain content with little. Nonetheless, however diminished your circumstances, if you are a stylist you will not only accept your situation but you will embrace it and make it part of your style.

And if you are a stylist you will enjoy the unique form of liberation which poverty makes possible. You will be liberated from the tyranny of possessions (which own you as much as you own them). Moreover, you will have the ultimate insurance policy: By having nothing, nothing can be taken from you. There will be no accountants or tax inspectors to deal with, no Joneses to keep up with. In short, you will understand why Mother Teresa, winner of the 1979 Nobel Peace Prize, had a ready answer when she was asked why so many women were eager to join her Missionaries of Charity. "It's the freedom of poverty," she said.

The greatest threat to that freedom is not solvency but indebtedness. It is easy to be solvent or indeed affluent with style, but it is almost impossible to be in debt with style. To borrow money is to sell some power over you to someone else, and thus to limit your freedom. Consequently, it is a transaction to be avoided at all costs. If you are in desperate need, ask for a gift instead of a loan. Or ask directly for that which you would buy with the money: food, clothing, shelter, etc. An outright donation is better for everyone concerned: It frees you from having to operate under a cloud of obligation, and it frees your benefactor from the resentments and suspicions aroused by conditional generosity.

Another threat to the "freedom of poverty" is the temptation to conceal or disguise your condition. Resist it. Not only is such masquerading a form of lying, but it also creates false assumptions about you that will inevitably be disappointed. Rather, you should parade your poverty, make it one of your trademarks—but always in such a way that it is not seen as a bid for sympathy or for charity. If you are very poor, the daily act of surviving will be both your triumph and your style.

One who has such style is a certain writer who lives in New York. He once lived in London, but wherever he has lived he has been acclaimed not for the genius of his prose style but for the genius of his life-style. Chronically impecunious, he survives by showing up at every party, reception, opening, convention, or any other type of gathering that features free food and drink. Using any of a number of different ruses to get in the door, he then engages everyone he can corner in a conversation brilliantly designed to elicit the times and whereabouts of future parties. He eats well.

But not as well as Jose Antonio Valencia, the celebrated Colombian gate-crasher whose exploits came to light in 1980 when the Dominican Republic's embassy in Bogotá was taken over by terrorists during a diplomatic reception. Among the guests held hostage was the charming and elegantly dressed Señor Valencia, who confessed to his captors that he was only at the party because party-going was his profession. While his confession has made him persona non grata at the embassy parties that were once his specialty, Señor Valencia still eats well. Now he has become a familiar figure at the funerals of wealthy strangers, where he sheds copious tears over the demise of the dear departed before tucking into the food.

Still, the most glorious example of wedding one's poverty to one's style was provided by a lady in wartime London, affectionately known to her friends in Soho's demimonde as the Countess. Regal of bearing and disdainful of charity, she wore her poverty as if it were a tiara. By day she would hold court in some dingy cafe, and by night she would sleep curled up in a steamer trunk on a bombsite. This latter fact, however, finally occasioned such concern among her friends that they took up a collection for her and then went to the bombsite one night in hopes of presenting her with the means of acquiring more comfortable accommodations. When they got there, one of them gently lifted the lid of the trunk and began explaining to her the purpose of their mission. Abruptly she interrupted. "Tell them I am not receiving at this hour," she said, and snatched the lid closed.

The Countess preferred the absolute freedom of absolute poverty to the more limited freedom that a little money buys. She understood, too, that poverty is territory. It is a kingdom in its own right, and the experience of living there confers on you a special fascination that you can get nowhere else. To come from Rome or Paris or London is far less interesting than to come from dire poverty. If you doubt this, ask yourself which anecdote would be more likely to arouse your interest—one that begins, "An amusing thing happened as I was driving down the Champs Elysées the other day, . . ." or one that begins, "An amusing thing happened as I was sleeping in the bus station last night. . . ."

So, to reverse the saying: If you haven't got anything, flaunt it. If your style is to be unencumbered by objects or obligations, revel in it.

What have you got to lose?

TEST YOUR STYLE QUOTIENT

1. If you are a stylist, you will avoid staying in shelters for the indigent because:

   (a) You consider yourself too good for them.
   (b) You consider yourself too wretched for them.

(c) You will have to sleep with strangers.

(d) You will become part of a group.

2. If you are a stylist, you will save your money because:

   (a) You want to improve your situation.

   (b) You want your children to have a better chance to become solvent.

   (c) You want to buy something useless.

   (d) You want to seem even poorer by not spending the money you have.

3. If you are a stylist, you will accept state charity because:

   (a) It will feed you.

   (b) You deserve it.

   (c) You don't deserve it.

   (d) It keeps bureaucrats employed and off the streets.

4. If you are a stylist, you will regret your poverty because:

   (a) It restricts your pleasure.

   (b) It restricts your movement.

   (c) It embarrasses your family.

   (d) It is hazardous to your health.

5. If you are a stylist, you will talk about your poverty because:

   (a) It is the most interesting thing about you.

   (b) It gives the other poor hope.

   (c) It gives the rich a guilty conscience.

   (d) It might elicit a gift.

(Answers on page 180)

BEING RICH

with Style

I T USED TO BE THAT GREAT
wealth, like great poverty, could be a style in itself. In fact,
in the Middle Ages wealth and style were so inextricably
bound up with one another that the rich kept all of their
gold and silver on permanent display in the entrance halls of
their houses so that visitors could immediately see precisely
what they were worth. And in the Renaissance great families
like the Medicis and the Borgias considered their wealth
almost as an aspect of their character.

Nowadays, however, wealth is so common and so widely
dispersed that the mere possession of it signifies little of interest. Indeed, it is often difficult to decide who is rich and
who isn't. J. Paul Getty, who was certainly qualified to speak
on the subject, once declared, "If you can actually count
your money you are not really a rich man." While that seems
a rather stern test to impose on those who would think of
themselves as rich, and was no doubt intended by Mr. Getty
to put distance between himself and other men of wealth,
it does indicate the near-futility today of depositing one's
style in one's bank account.

In any event, it is as foolish to base your style on your
money as it is to base it on your beauty or your job, for if

you ever lose your money (or your beauty or your job) you lose your style along with it.

Obviously, then, as far as your style is concerned, it is not the amount of money you have but what you do with it that matters. Consider the case of the Kennedys. John Kennedy used his money to buy himself a presidency, and then used the presidency as a vehicle for the expression of his style. Excellent. Jacqueline Kennedy, on the other hand, did precisely the opposite. She drained her reservoir of style for the sole purpose of acquiring money, and more money, and still more money. She succeeded, if you can call it that, but she paid a fearful price. Not only did she end up without style, she ended up living with Aristotle Onassis and working for Doubleday.

Thus did the Kennedys, in their different ways, prove the truth of Sir Francis Bacon's axiom: "Riches are a good handmaid, but the worst mistress."

There is no point in having or acquiring riches unless they are put to good use. A stylist would never accumulate or hoard wealth simply to keep it lying around like a mistress, to give pleasure by its very presence. Being rich with style really means spending money with style.

As it is your style we are concerned with here, not your comfort or security or status, it follows that your money is best spent on things which enhance that style. For example, anything that gives you wider experience or exposure—such as travel, which does both—is a good investment. (This is particularly true when you are young and still in your experimental phase as a stylist.) Beyond that, anything that gives you happiness is worth spending money on. The notion that money can't buy you happiness is a fallacy. As a matter of fact, happiness is about the *only* important thing that money can buy. It can't buy you style, or intelligence, or beauty, or wit, or affection, or respect, but it can definitely buy you happiness.

Sir Alexander Korda, the distinguished film producer, used to buy himself a great deal of happiness in the form of caviar, which he consumed daily in large quantities. His explanation: "One can be unhappy before eating caviar, even after, but at least not *during.*" Nor was his stylish extravagance lavished only on himself. He once stopped the filming of *An Ideal Husband* and ordered a $460,000 diamond necklace for Paulette Goddard to wear in the movie. The reason? "It makes her feel better," he shrugged. In the same vein, after his son Vincent was born, John Jacob Astor IV had all the streets around their Fifth Avenue mansion covered with straw because the clatter of carriages disturbed his wife's rest.

Truly, as Dr. Johnson observed, it is better to live rich than to die rich.

Still, living rich *with style* requires more than just the ability to spend money on yourself. It also requires the ability to recognize when *not* to spend money. In this context you would do well to heed the advice of Maurice Rheims, France's leading art auctioneer, who wrote at the end of his memoirs, "Distrust objects." As we mentioned in the last chapter, objects which you possess tend, in time, to possess you.

Therefore, you should only buy objects which complement and express your style, objects which you plan to use and enjoy. For instance, if you buy porcelain which you only bring out for "special" occasions, or which you are afraid to put through the dishwasher, you are not adding anything to your style. You are merely adding to your clutter, which gets in the way of your style.

Nor does a stylist ever buy something purely for the sake of owning it. Besides being nonsensical, it is the unmistakable mark of someone who values himself for what he has rather than for what he is. Maurice Rothschild was such a person. After his father Edmond died, he fought with his brothers and sisters for fifteen years over the ownership of an ancient casket that was in the collection left by his father. Yet when he finally got it, he put it in a bank vault and never looked at it again.

That may seem an extreme example of ownership for the sake of ownership, but it is only slightly more bizarre than buying a piece of jewelry and then keeping it locked away in a safe-deposit box. Which brings us to one of the cardinal principles of spending money with style: Never buy anything which you are not willing to discard later. If an object is so desirable that its loss or destruction is liable to cause you great distress, then to buy it is to mortgage your future happiness, and perhaps even your self-control. That's one condition of sale you should never accept.

It is a mistake, too, to buy bigger or fancier or more expensive versions of things you already have just because you have the money to do so. If something you own is right for your style—and if it's not, why do you have it?—then it is foolish to spend your money replacing it unless, of course, the new acquisition is even more right for your style. It is a typical gaffe of the nouveau riche to acquire something not because it reveals an aspect of your personality, but simply because it shows you can afford it.

Speaking of the nouveau riche, it should be said that the problems of being rich with style pale in comparison to the problems of *becoming* rich with style. When St. Matthew wrote that it is easier for a camel to go through the eye of a needle than for a rich man to enter into the Kingdom of God, it was not a person's wealth that troubled the apostle so much as how he came by it. For as Terry Southern sought to depict in *The Magic Christian,* where dollars were planted in a swamp of excrement, people will go to quite amazing lengths to get their hands on money. And since all the money not now in your hands is in someone else's hands, the temptations to shed your style in the pursuit of wealth are powerful indeed.

Yet they can be overcome so long as you don't think of the acquisition of wealth as a means to an end, but rather as another expression of your personality—a part of your style, in other words. Rich people with style don't suddenly stop making profitable business deals just because they have "enough" money, or because they have "retired." They continue as before because their special genius is for making money, and not to exercise that genius would be to deny a crucial element in their style.

It should be emphasized, however, that a genius for making money, like any other genius, is a matter of luck rather than virtue. This doesn't mean that you don't deserve your money—you always deserve what you get—but it does mean that you shouldn't make the mistake of thinking you *earned* it. You may have worked hard for it, but if hard work determined the level of one's compensation migrant farm laborers would all be plutocrats. Becoming rich has nothing to do with being justly rewarded for your labor and has everything to do with being in the right place at the right time with the right ideas and the right aptitude (or connections) for exploiting the right opportunities. The reason that we stress this point is that if you think otherwise—that is, if you actually believe that you earned your money starting from scratch, or anywhere near it—such thinking will lead you so far down the road of self-delusion that your style will have been irretrievably lost long before you ever have the chance to be both rich and stylish.

It should also be borne in mind that to be rich with style is to scrupulously avoid the subject of your wealth as a topic of conversation. While you undoubtedly don't need to be told that it's vulgar and boring to allude *directly* to your wealth, you should still be on guard against bringing it up indirectly. There are many subtle ways of implying the presence of wealth without actually mentioning it—by complaining about the high level of your taxes, for instance, or expressing dismay at the cost of private schools for your children, or moaning about the difficulty of finding reliable servants—all of which can be as damaging to your style as if you had come right out with a statement of your assets.

At the same time, you should never pretend that you are *not* wealthy. Any reference to your limited means that is plainly contradicted by your circumstances will be seen as either an upside-down boast or a simple lie. Both are offensive. And, again, you must take care not to *imply* that your money is in shorter supply than it really is—by talking about the bargains you can find at Woolworth's, for example, or the merits of taking the bus instead of a taxi. Such misleading hints diminish your credibility rather than your wealth in the eyes of others.

Above all, you must not feel guilty about being rich. Feelings of guilt are fruitless and dispiriting even in cases where they might conceivably be justified. But in the case of wealth, which can easily be disposed of if it is so burdensome, such feelings are contemptible as well, because they are hypocritical. If you are embarrassed that you have a chauffeured limousine, get rid of it. Don't try to justify it by claiming that it is only to enable you to get more work done outside the office. Likewise, if you are like Jimmy Carter was and you're uneasy with the special perquisites that come with your job, change jobs. Don't go around carrying your own garment bag to try to show that you're "regular folks."

If you are going to be rich with style, you must be as

comfortable with your wealth and as unselfconscious about it as was the late Nubar Gulbenkian, a man whose fortune was matched only by his capacity for enjoying it. Indeed, not only did Gulbenkian enjoy his wealth, he enjoyed disappointing those who wanted to see some evidence that would disprove Scott Fitzgerald's assertion that the rich are different from other people. Instead he reaffirmed it, teasingly and often, by expounding publicly on such matters as the great advantage of London taxis: "They can turn on a sixpence," he would say, adding with a twinkle, "whatever that is."

Alas, not many of the rich can contemplate their wealth with the serenity that Gulbenkian did (perhaps because they know where it came from). Thus are they often driven to atone for the guilt of being rich by acts of public philanthropy. This is a terrible mistake. Philanthropy—by which we mean the organized and publicized doling out of endowments and grants as opposed to private generosity—is perhaps the ultimate exercise in hypocrisy. It is merely a way of laundering your image, a cynical attempt to get people to remember how you gave away your money rather than how you got it. It is no coincidence that so many of the biggest philanthropic foundations were established by the worst robber barons.

We are not arguing here against charity. On the contrary, the ability to be charitable is one of the great pleasures of being rich. What is contemptible and styleless is bogus charity—charity primarily designed to bring glory to your name rather than to bring aid to the needy.

So if you are rich enough to be able to give away money on a large scale, remember that there is only one way to do it with style: personally, directly, unconditionally. And remember, too, that there is only one worthy cause: people.

If being rich with style is really spending money with style, you will not find anything better to spend your money on than people—first yourself, and then others.

TEST YOUR
STYLE QUOTIENT

1. If you are a stylist, you will apologize for your wealth because:

   (a) You don't want to provoke resentment.
   (b) You did nothing to earn it.
   (c) You want to put the less fortunate at ease.
   (d) You wish you had more.

2. If you are a stylist, you will not employ servants because:

   (a) They don't do things as well as you.
   (b) Their manners are generally better than yours.
   (c) They force you into the role of a boss.
   (d) They invade your privacy.

3. If you are a stylist, you will patronize inexpensive shops because:

   (a) You see no point in wasting money.
   (b) You prefer the merchandise.
   (c) You have a reputation for finding bargains.
   (d) The shops happen to be nearby.

4. If you are a stylist, you will leave your fortune to a stranger because:

(*a*) You want to demonstrate the unimportance of your wealth.

(*b*) You want to make a grand gesture.

(*c*) You want to repay a kindness.

(*d*) You want to repay your relatives for neglecting you.

5. If you are a stylist, you will talk about your wealth because:

(*a*) You have been paid to.

(*b*) You want people to know how you got it.

(*c*) You want people to know how much you have so as to cheer up your creditors.

(*d*) You want people to know how little you have so as to discourage would-be borrowers.

(Answers on page 180)

BEING SHADY

with Style

WHEN WE REMEMBER ALL
of the attributes that go into the making of a stylist, it becomes readily apparent that there are two distinct groups of people who are virtually precluded from having style: politicians and criminals. (Actually, as recent political history has taught us, the two groups are more distinct from the rest of us than they are from each other.)

The reason that politicians with style are such rarities—in a democratic society, that is—is that, first of all, their survival as politicians depends on winning the approval of others. And no stylist is ever concerned about winning other people's approval. Secondly, a democratic politician is by definition a representative of the people who elected him, whereas a stylist represents nobody but himself. Moreover, as any group is inherently lacking in style, to represent them effectively is to be a spokesman for their stylessness. A politician is also obliged to keep checking the public opinion polls to find out what people are thinking so that he can act accordingly. A stylist, in contrast, is never guided in his actions by the opinions of others.

When you add to all this the definition of a stylist as someone who is truthful, sincere, consistent, and noncompetitive, you begin to see the near impossibility of a politician ever having style.

Nevertheless, there *are* things a politician can do to overcome the natural handicaps of his profession and achieve style. Perhaps the most important is to cultivate his oratorical skills; there have been few stylish politicians who were not also accomplished speakers. The ability to make a great speech will compensate for just about any shortcoming. And when making a speech, a politician with style will resist the urge to tell his listeners what they want to hear. He will not arouse expectations that he cannot fulfill. Indeed, the great political stylists have usually taken the contrary approach and called for sacrifice, as John Kennedy did ("Ask not what your country can do for you . . .") and before him Winston Churchill ("I have nothing to offer but blood, toil, tears, and sweat . . .").

Nor does the politician with style ever try to justify himself when his performance fails to live up to his rhetoric. One of the most unedifying spectacles of recent years, for example, was the frantic effort by President Carter to exculpate himself with regard to the wreckage of the economy. Beginning with the third year of his presidency, when the country sank into a recession at the same time that inflation rose to three times the level it had been when he took office, Mr. Carter adopted as his chief domestic policy a frenzy of finger-pointing, blaming his troubles on OPEC, cabinet officials, Congress, and finally the American people as a whole. Now contrast this with the splendid reaction of Huey Long, a man of some style as well as much guile, when he was asked by his worried press secretary how he should respond to accusations that Long had failed to keep his campaign promises. The Kingfish's reply was a classic: "Fuck 'em. Tell 'em I lied."

Like a stylist in any other walk of life, the stylist in politics must also be prepared to offer up his private life to public scrutiny—even more so in politics because by becoming a politician you automatically turn yourself into public property. Therefore you must either conduct yourself at all times in a manner of which the voters approve, or be ready to accept the consequences when the word gets out, as it surely will, that you like to enjoy yourself in ways displeasing to much of the electorate. In fact, it is best not to wait until the word gets out, but to put it out yourself. Self-accusations are always the easiest to deal with. In any case, when faced with accusations or the threat of imminent revelations, it is a grave error to try to cover your tracks. This is what John Profumo did with Christine Keeler, and Senator Kennedy did with Mary Jo Kopechne, and British Liberal Party leader Jeremy Thorpe did with his alleged homosexual lover Norman Scott—and they all paid for it with their style.

Another problem confronting the politician is that if he is to perform his job with style he must not only impose his personality on his job, like any other stylist, but he must also impose his personality, his vision, on the constituency he represents. This is true whether one is the mayor of a small town or the leader of a great nation. David Ben-Gurion may have been stubborn and self-righteous and implacable in his Zionism, but he had the style to shape the state of Israel in his own image. Likewise, Charles de Gaulle may have antagonized half the world with his arrogance and hauteur, but he had the style to reinvent France as a uniquely Gaullist creation.

The final problem with which a politician must cope if he is to have any claim on style comes the day when he is forced to relinquish his office. Because every political career is sustained by regular doses of public approval, when that approval is withdrawn the feeling of rejection can turn even the coolest of politicians into confused, embittered has-beens.

This is why the moment of leaving office is as revealing of a politician's style as the moment of taking office.

As with the possession of objects, one should never take possession of an office if one is not prepared to give it up with equanimity. Even the most stylish performance as a public officeholder can be swiftly blotted out by the sight of a defeated candidate either choking on self-pity or snarling about his "enemies." It is a measure of Richard Nixon's awesome stylelessness that after almost demolishing his career in one stroke in 1962 with his graceless performance at the press conference following his defeat in the California gubernatorial election, he then embarked on an arduous and determined political comeback only to repeat the performance in 1974.

Of course the best way to leave the political stage is with a brief flourish the moment you hear the audience starting to murmur and fidget. But for most politicians, who yearn to hear the cries of "Encore!" just one more time, such a triumph of timing requires almost superhuman sensitivity. So perhaps that is expecting too much of anyone. Still, it is not too much to expect a politician with style to prepare himself for an early curtain by having ready a statement that at least approximates in eloquence, concision, and humor the magnificent concession speech delivered a few years ago by political prankster Dick Tuck, after he had been trounced in his bid to become a California state assemblyman. After thanking his supporters, Mr. Tuck solemnly declared: "The people have spoken—the bastards."

If politicians are forced to labor under the burden of having to please most of the people most of the time, criminals who would be stylists suffer from the opposite but equally crippling handicap of having to avoid attracting the attention of most of the people most of the time. Whereas stylists are distinguished by having nothing to hide, criminals are noted for having everything to hide—including often themselves.

Yet there *have* been criminals with style. And they have all had three things in common which marked them off from ordinary criminals. In the first place, they all pursued a criminal career not because they were poor and needed the money but because they were good at it. They had a vocation for law-breaking. Secondly, their crimes bore the stamp of their personality. They always left their distinctive mark on their misdeeds (sometimes quite literally: there was an Italian counterfeiter of ancient Roman bronzes who actually put his own tiny hallmark on each forgery). And thirdly, they remained outlaws to the end. Just like people with a flair for legitimate business, they didn't cease their activities simply because they had enough money to retire.

Mafia don Joseph Bonanno is an excellent example of a criminal stylist who has remained determinedly unretired well into his seventies. Although he supposedly gave up his gangland activities when he moved to Tucson in 1966, after rival Mafia bosses strongly hinted that the only way he would live to a ripe old age would be in retirement, it was only a matter of a few years before he had taken over Arizona's mob rackets and had set up a chain of companies that today controls the mozzarella cheese business throughout North America. You can't keep a bad man down.

Nor is Bonanno unique among his colleagues. Mafiosi generally have more style than other underworld figures because they are, to the extent that prudence allows, usually forthright and open—audacious even—about their unsavory role in the economy.

Of course that style was set by the master himself, Al Capone. Old Scarface freely admitted that he was a bootlegger among other things, although he was happy to point out that his liquor was only bootleg when it was on the trucks.

"When it reaches you on a silver tray in your club," he added, "it's hospitality." Indeed, to hear Capone tell it, his gangsterism was a form of patriotism. "My rackets are run on strictly American lines," he once boasted, "and they're going to stay that way."

No discussion of shady types would be complete without some mention of those people whose devotion to the shade is such that we might refer to them as the vanishing species. That is, they are people who specialize in vanishing. As you might expect, the stylists among them are few and far between—it is not easy to base one's style on staying out of sight—but the fact that there *are* people who have disappeared with style shows that no human activity can be considered totally style-resistant.

The key to vanishing with style is to make yourself invisible in such a way that the world reverberates with your absence. You cannot play peek-a-boo with the world, as Greta Garbo and T. E. Lawrence used to do, or as Abbie Hoffman did, teasingly, until he resurfaced in 1980. Nor can you issue bulletins on your reclusion, as John Lennon and Yoko Ono did in 1979 with their full-page advertisement in *The New York Times*. Nor can you offer occasional glimpses of yourself, as J. D. Salinger does from time to time.

If you want to vanish with style, you must leave behind a vacuum so absolute and so dramatic that the world will be forever tantalized by your withdrawal from it.

This is what airplane hijacker D. B. Cooper did a few years ago when he parachuted out of the public eye clutching a bag full of ransom money. Equally stylish, if less spectacular, were the exits of Ambrose Bierce, Judge Crater, and Martin Bormann. But of course the supreme stylist at taking himself hostage was Howard Hughes, who for twenty years was the world's most conspicuous tycoon by remaining maddeningly invisible.

If Hughes was the undisputed master of the vanishing act, it was left to an artist named Lee Lozano to raise it to the level of an art form. In the mid-seventies Lozano announced that his next work would be entitled *General Strike Piece,* and to execute it he would "gradually but determinedly avoid being present at official or public functions or gatherings related to the 'art world'."

Judged by the artist's stated intentions, the work was a masterpiece. Lozano has not been seen since.

TEST YOUR STYLE QUOTIENT

1. If you are a stylist, you will run for political office because:

   (a) You need a job.
   (b) You need an audience.
   (c) You want to serve the people.
   (d) You want to rule the world.

2. If you are a stylist, you will make false promises to the electorate because:

   (a) The electorate wants promises, and you don't know yet which ones are false.
   (b) You know they are false, but they are so well phrased.
   (c) You want to find out how bright the voters are.
   (d) You want to get their attention.

3. If you are a stylist, and if you have the power, you will have your political opponents imprisoned because:

   (a) They get on your nerves.
   (b) They will be better people for the experience.

(c) They would do the same to you.

(d) You are curious to see if you can get away with it.

4. If you are a stylist who is also a convicted criminal, you will attempt to escape from jail because:

(a) You said you would.

(b) It breaks the monotony.

(c) You don't like prison.

(d) You never stay in one place for long.

5. If you are a stylist, you will vanish from sight because:

(a) You want to get away from it all.

(b) Someone is after you.

(c) You know you won't be missed.

(d) You know you will be missed.

(Answers on page 180)

BEING OLD

with Style

JONATHAN SWIFT SUMMED UP
best the ambivalence we all feel about aging: "Every man
desires to live long, but no man would be old."

For most people old age is simultaneously a blessing and
a curse, a condition one accepts only because it is preferable
to the alternative. Yet for the stylist there are definite advantages to being old. To begin with, as you have been in
the same role for quite a while, by now your style should
come to you as naturally as breathing. In addition, as you
are getting toward the end of your run, you are free to over-
act. Your statement about yourself has already been made;
now you can underline it.

Also, because less is expected of you when you are old,
you can get away with more. No one is threatened or made
suspicious if you go to extremes in expressing your style,
because old age itself is one of life's extremes. You have the
ultimate luxury of *being* without the burdensome necessity
of *doing* something. In short, your later years should be the
golden age of your style.

The reason that most people find old age a greater trial
than they had bargained for is that most people devote their
lives to doing and only secondarily, if at all, to being, with
the result that when the time comes for them to cease doing

there is a sense of loss rather than a sense of liberation. In his book, *The View in Winter,* Ronald Blythe quotes an elderly Anglican monk as saying that in old age "the lesson to be learnt is to understand the promotion from plum-easy doing to the surprisingly difficult non-activity of just *being.*" That is a lesson the stylist learns long before he reaches old age.

There are, nevertheless, pitfalls peculiar to old age which even the stylist must take care to avoid. One is the temptation to dwell on (and to try to dwell *in*) the past. The past may be a rich source of anecdotes, but it is a poor source of inspiration for coping with the present. That's what you have your style for.

If retreating into the past is a bad idea, trying to pro-long the present is even worse. For centuries, thanks to a combination of Christian and capitalist theology (whereby you were promised a raise in the hereafter), together with the primitive state of medical technology, people were happy to accept that their days on earth were strictly numbered. Now, however, that Christianity and capitalism have lost some of their grip, while medicine has made startling advances, people are less willing to accept that their earthly leasehold has run out. So they turn themselves over to the doctors (some of whom are little better than witch doctors) in hopes of negotiating an extension.

This is a horrendous mistake. First of all, it shows that you are panicky, and panic is not in the stylist's emotional repertoire. Secondly, it shows that you calculate the value of your life according to the actuarial tables—the longer it is, the better—whereas your style has nothing whatever to do with your life span. Thirdly, it shows that you have so little regard for yourself that you are willing to become an advertisement for a doctor's style. (Look at the lugubrious examples of Charles Lindbergh, Thomas Mann, Konrad Adenauer, Pope

Pius XII, and Somerset Maugham, all of whom spent their last days not as monuments to the durability of their style but as monuments to the success—or failure—of Dr. Paul Niehans's "rejuvenation therapy.") And, fourthly, it shows that you are willing to risk the style-destroying effects of senility, for it is very common for the body, given any encouragement, to keep functioning long after the mind has shut down for good. Thus Somerset Maugham, in his late eighties, was still able to have an erection, as he never tired of demonstrating to friends, but his speech consisted mostly of demented babbling. That is not the way to go.

Of course you may know that *now*, but you won't know it later when your mind actually begins to play tricks on you. "After all," Gore Vidal has pointed out, "as you lose your marbles you don't know that you haven't still got the full complement. So you are apt to think yourself cute as a bug's ear long after all the others have tiptoed from the room."

So don't go to any special trouble to stretch out your life. It's quite enough to follow Sophie Tucker's advice, when she was asked to account for her longevity: "Keep breathing."

Also, as you get on in years, you should be careful not to do anything that you wouldn't be caught dead doing. Don't let the Grim Reaper catch you with your pants down, as he did Nelson Rockefeller, who expired while exerting himself with his blonde assistant—an embarrassment which prompted one obituarist to comment, "Rockefeller slipped out of life on a banana peel." Another who exited on a banana peel was the nutritionist J. I. Rodale. The seventy-two-year-old Rodale, who constantly boasted that he would live to be a hundred because of his sugar-free diet, was appearing on "The Dick Cavett Show" to tell the world the secret of his good health when he dropped dead in mid-sentence.

Finally, if you can possibly avoid it, you should never

waste any part of your old age in a nursing home. A nursing home is nothing more than a club where group dying is practiced. As has already been made clear, it is a bad idea at the best of times to identify yourself in terms of a group, but to associate yourself with a group whose sole claim to fame is their imminent extinction is positively grotesque.

As being old with style involves the recognition that you may stop being old at any minute, we should say a few words about dying with style. And the words should be taken seriously, because if you don't get it right the first time you will almost certainly not get a second chance. As Molière put it, "We die only once, and for such a long time!"

If you are one of the lucky few, death will catch you in the act that you have spent most of your life perfecting. Houdini died thus, from a ruptured appendix as a result of a vicious punch to the midsection which he had casually invited, because such invitations were part of his routine. Similarly, Karl Wallenda, the septuagenarian head of the family of Flying Wallendas, flew to his death when a sudden wind toppled him from the high wire he was walking. But Isadora Duncan was perhaps the luckiest of all, for she was able to manage not only a typically dramatic exit, but also with an appropriately dramatic exit line. The end came on a chilly September day in Paris in 1927, as Miss Duncan was about to test-drive a red Bugatti that she wanted to buy. Having chosen to wear a long scarf instead of a coat for such a *sportif* occasion, she flung the scarf back over her shoulder with a grand gesture and bade her friends farewell. "Adieu, mes amis," she called out, "je vais à la gloire." And she did. As she drove away, her scarf got caught in the car's wheel spokes and snapped her neck. She died instantly.

If dying is an art, as Sylvia Plath once said, then the artistry involved depends first on your sense of timing. Unfortunately, however, most people don't hear their cue to move offstage (unlike most animals, who seem to know instinctively when their time is up and quickly, quietly drop out of sight). One of the few people who did hear, apparently, was the journalist Ambrose Bierce, who went to Mexico in 1913 at the age of seventy-one and disappeared. He was ill at the time and, according to his daughter Helen, "When his hour struck he wanted to go quickly and with none of his friends near to look upon his face afterward."

It takes style to do what Bierce did, to end your life in effect. It takes style *and* courage to end it in fact. But that is the only way to be certain that you don't fall victim to either the humiliation of the banana peel or the slow torture of gradual incapacitation.

You, and you alone, can put an exclamation mark after your life's sentence.

To make that mark with maximum effectiveness, you must make it in a manner consistent with your style. Sarah Bernhardt, for example, in a failed suicide attempt early in her career, tried to poison herself by drinking liquid rouge. Ernest Hemingway, the Great White Hunter who had shot just about everything that moves, shot himself. Virginia Woolf, the author of *The Voyage Out, To The Lighthouse,* and *The Waves,* drowned herself. And Yukio Mishima, the author who celebrated the samurai ideal, disemboweled himself prior to being decapitated, in the tradition of the Japanese warrior.

Others have rejected the definitive final stroke in favor of what might be called suicide by omission. These are people who deliberately failed to change their style even if by doing so they could have coaxed a few more years out of their bodies. Kenneth Tynan was a lifelong chain-smoker who continued to smoke heavily even after he discovered he had emphysema. (Upon Tynan's death, at fifty-three, fellow drama critic John Simon wrote: "Even the illness that took his breath away seemed to be imitating him—with his wit, elegance, and versatility he had always taken away ours.") Edgar Allan Poe and Dylan Thomas, both epic drinkers, chose to go out of life on a colossal binge. And Tycho Brahe, the Danish astronomer who was renowned for his good manners, died in 1601 at the age of fifty-five solely because he put his manners above his health. During the course of a banquet in Prague, Brahe found himself in increasing pain because he had neglected to relieve himself beforehand, yet he made no mention of it nor left the table because he thought it would be ill-mannered to do so. He died several days later of a burst bladder.

Dying with style, then, is most often a do-it-yourself enterprise. So why does suicide continue to have a bad name? Partly it has to do with its having been anathematized by the Church, but mostly it is because people self-destruct for the wrong reasons and in the wrong ways. Heading the list of wrong reasons is despondency. To commit suicide because you are despondent is not to take control of your fate but to *surrender* control to the very forces that have caused your unhappiness. Also at the top of the list of wrong reasons to do yourself in is revenge, the desire to get back at someone, or the world at large, for mistreating you. Like everything else a stylist does, suicide is a statement about yourself, not about others.

Among the wrong ways to commit suicide is any way that is fashionable. In the sixties, for example, it became fashionable for students at Berkeley to drop out of school by flinging themselves off the university's campanile. (The fashion subsided only after someone painted a bull's-eye on the concrete at the foot of the tower.) The poor students obviously had no sense of style, for it is as styleless to try to die fashionably as it is to try to live fashionably. It is a mistake, too, to try to end your life in a way that could easily fail. A failed suicide is always seen, rightly or not, as a bid for sympathy or for pity, neither of which a stylist wants.

Nor does a stylist ever seek to explain or justify his climactic action. The action speaks for itself. The New York lady who in 1979 gave a "suicide party" so that she could say goodbye to her family and friends and explain to them the reasons for calling her own number, and who went to the trouble and expense of having the whole tear-stained affair videotaped, succeeded not in dignifying her decision but only in producing an obscene comic opera. If you want to say goodbye, do it the way the poet Hart Crane did it when he leapt overboard from a ship in the Caribbean. "Goodbye, everybody!" he shouted.

Likewise, if you feel the need to leave behind an explanatory farewell message, it should be kept brief and unsentimental. The more you write, the greater the danger that you will slide into mawkishness or self-pity or even accusation. The model suicide note is concise and to the point, like the one left on a bedside table by George Eastman, the inventor of the Kodak camera, who died at eighty-eight of a drug overdose. The note read simply: "Why wait?"

That says it all.

Finally, there is one other bit of writing you can do toward the end which will materially affect your style after you have departed: the writing of your will. This is your last chance to design the shape of the memory people will have of you, and if you use it cleverly you can do a lot to sharpen and perpetuate the image you have spent your life creating. On the other hand, if you squander it, for instance by taking the opportunity to deliver posthumous judgments on the people you leave behind, you will have signed away your claim on style.

If your will is to be the final documentation of your

style it must bear the imprint of your personality. It should be written so that when it is made public people will nod and say, "How typical!" The strongly militaristic Peter the Great, for example, put into his will a complete plan of strategy for the Russian conquest of Europe. On a more frivolous note, Sir Francis Laking, a playboy and practical joker who died in 1930 after drinking too much yellow chartreuse, bequeathed all his cars to his friend Tallulah Bankhead. Sir Francis did not own any cars.

Then there was the flamboyant widow of a Texas oil millionaire who decided to take her car with her. She stipulated in her will that she was to be buried in her lace nightgown "in my Ferrari, with the seat slanted comfortably." Maxine Elliott, the former actress who had been a close friend of Edward VII, was another who wanted to carry on in death as she had in life. And since she had always lied about her age, she left instructions that the birthdate on her tombstone should be moved up by eleven years.

But for the most extraordinary example of posthumous style we must turn to a series of documents left by the mother of the French novelist Romain Gary (who himself committed suicide in 1980). During World War II, while her son was away fighting with the Free French air force, she realized that she was about to die. Not wishing to cause her son distress at a time when he needed hope and encouragement, she thereupon sat down and began writing him hundreds of letters. These letters were then turned over to a friend with the instructions that after her death one letter was to be mailed every day until the end of the war. Thus when Romain Gary returned home after the war as a decorated hero, he found that his mother and faithful correspondent had been dead for two years.

If medals were given for style, Romain Gary's mother might well be the most decorated hero of them all. For, in the end, style is a way of sending a message, a message that gets through regardless of the circumstances.

And it is a message that, once delivered, stays with people long after you're gone.

TEST YOUR
STYLE QUOTIENT

1. If you are a stylist, you will change your dress style in old age because:

   (a) You want to look your age.
   (b) You want to shock your remaining contemporaries.
   (c) You want a new image.
   (d) You have spotted a flaw in your old image.

2. If you are a stylist, you will talk about the good old days because:

   (a) Everyone else is.
   (b) There is no one in the room.
   (c) You have been asked to.
   (d) You want to rehearse anecdotes for your memoirs.

3. If you are a stylist, you will go to Mexico or Switzerland for medical treatment because:

   (a) You want to be cured of your ailments.
   (b) You want to cure Mexico or Switzerland of its ailments.
   (c) You have been invited to make a speech while you are there.
   (d) You have run out of things to spend money on.

4. If you are a stylist, you will "accidentally" fall in front of a swiftly moving car because:

   (a) You want to die a spectacular death.
   (b) It's cheaper than buying the drugs for an overdose.
   (c) It outwits the insurance company.
   (d) It will be more widely talked about than a "natural" death.

5. If you are a stylist, you will refuse to make a will because:

   (a) You are not of sound mind and body.
   (b) You don't plan to leave anything.
   (c) You wish to make a point of not giving employment to lawyers.
   (d) You are amused by the idea of your greedy relatives quarreling with each other after you are gone.

(Answers on page 180)

ANSWERS TO
THE STYLE
QUOTIENT TESTS

T<small>HE HIGHEST SCORE YOU CAN</small> receive on each question is 3, the lowest 0. Therefore if your aggregate score for any one chapter is from 12 to 15, you can definitely consider yourself a stylist in that area. If you score in the 6 to 11 range, you have a sense of style but it needs refining. If you score below 6, you would do well to reread the chapter.

To find your overall Style Quotient, total your scores for all of the chapters. If your score is 150 or over, you are a certified stylistic genius. If it is 75 or over, you have promise as a stylist, but you will have to work to develop it. If you scored under 75, at least you had the sense to buy just the right book for you.

DRESSING
WITH STYLE

1.		2.		3.		4.		5.	
(a)	2	(a)	1	(a)	2	(a)	1	(a)	2
(b)	3	(b)	1	(b)	1	(b)	2	(b)	2
(c)	1	(c)	3	(c)	3	(c)	0	(c)	1
(d)	1	(d)	2	(d)	0	(d)	3	(d)	3

SPEAKING
WITH STYLE

	1.		2.		3.		4.		5.	
(a)	2	*(a)*	2	*(a)*	0	*(a)*	2	*(a)*	0
(b)	3	*(b)*	0	*(b)*	1	*(b)*	0	*(b)*	2
(c)	1	*(c)*	3	*(c)*	2	*(c)*	3	*(c)*	3
(d)	1	*(d)*	1	*(d)*	3	*(d)*	1	*(d)*	1

EATING AND DRINKING
WITH STYLE

	1.		2.		3.		4.		5.	
(a)	1	*(a)*	1	*(a)*	0	*(a)*	1	*(a)*	0
(b)	2	*(b)*	0	*(b)*	2	*(b)*	0	*(b)*	0
(c)	1	*(c)*	2	*(c)*	1	*(c)*	2	*(c)*	2
(d)	3	*(d)*	3	*(d)*	3	*(d)*	3	*(d)*	3

MATING AND MARRYING
WITH STYLE

	1.		2.		3.		4.		5.	
(a)	0	*(a)*	1	*(a)*	2	*(a)*	3	*(a)*	1
(b)	2	*(b)*	0	*(b)*	3	*(b)*	0	*(b)*	3
(c)	3	*(c)*	3	*(c)*	0	*(c)*	2	*(c)*	0
(d)	1	*(d)*	2	*(d)*	1	*(d)*	1	*(d)*	2

CREATING A HOME
WITH STYLE

	1.		2.		3.		4.		5.	
(a)	0	*(a)*	0	*(a)*	1	*(a)*	0	*(a)*	0
(b)	1	*(b)*	0	*(b)*	0	*(b)*	1	*(b)*	3
(c)	3	*(c)*	2	*(c)*	3	*(c)*	3	*(c)*	2
(d)	2	*(d)*	3	*(d)*	2	*(d)*	2	*(d)*	1

CREATING A FAMILY
WITH STYLE

1. *(a)* 0	2. *(a)* 1	3. *(a)* 3	4. *(a)* 2	5. *(a)* 0
(b) 1	*(b)* 2	*(b)* 1	*(b)* 3	*(b)* 2
(c) 2	*(c)* 0	*(c)* 0	*(c)* 3	*(c)* 3
(d) 3	*(d)* 3	*(d)* 1	*(d)* 0	*(d)* 2

PERFORMING YOUR JOB
WITH STYLE

1. *(a)* 1	2. *(a)* 0	3. *(a)* 0	4. *(a)* 3	5. *(a)* 3
(b) 0	*(b)* 3	*(b)* 3	*(b)* 0	*(b)* 1
(c) 2	*(c)* 2	*(c)* 1	*(c)* 2	*(c)* 0
(d) 3	*(d)* 1	*(d)* 1	*(d)* 1	*(d)* 2

ENTERTAINING YOUR FRIENDS
WITH STYLE

1. *(a)* 3	2. *(a)* 0	3. *(a)* 3	4. *(a)* 1	5. *(a)* 0
(b) 2	*(b)* 3	*(b)* 0	*(b)* 2	*(b)* 3
(c) 0	*(c)* 1	*(c)* 2	*(c)* 0	*(c)* 2
(d) 1	*(d)* 2	*(d)* 1	*(d)* 3	*(d)* 2

CONFUSING YOUR ENEMIES
WITH STYLE

1. *(a)* 0	2. *(a)* 0	3. *(a)* 0	4. *(a)* 0	5. *(a)* 0
(b) 3	*(b)* 2	*(b)* 1	*(b)* 3	*(b)* 1
(c) 1	*(c)* 0	*(c)* 2	*(c)* 2	*(c)* 2
(d) 2	*(d)* 3	*(d)* 3	*(d)* 0	*(d)* 3

BEING POOR
WITH STYLE

	1.	2.	3.	4.	5.
(a)	0	0	2	1	3
(b)	2	1	1	3	1
(c)	1	3	3	0	0
(d)	3	2	0	2	2

BEING RICH
WITH STYLE

	1.	2.	3.	4.	5.
(a)	1	3	0	3	3
(b)	0	0	3	2	0
(c)	2	2	2	0	1
(d)	3	1	1	1	1

BEING SHADY
WITH STYLE

	1.	2.	3.	4.	5.
(a)	1	1	2	3	2
(b)	3	2	1	1	0
(c)	0	2	0	1	1
(d)	2	3	3	2	3

BEING OLD
WITH STYLE

	1.	2.	3.	4.	5.
(a)	2	0	0	2	1
(b)	1	1	1	1	0
(c)	0	3	3	2	3
(d)	3	2	2	3	2

INDEX